Conquering Burnout in a Toxic Workplace

Techniques for Transforming Stress and Escaping Anxiety So You Can Stay Motivated and Take Control of Your Career

Alison Flickinger

CONTENTS

DEDICATION

This book is dedicated to my friend and former co-worker Kevin, who in part, tragically lost his life to a toxic boss and workplace. His passing, along with my own experiences in several toxic workplaces, haunted me for years and made me realize the disturbing prevalence of this issue. So many of us spend the majority of our lives at work, and it's unacceptable to endure such destructive situations on a daily basis.

Years after Kevin's death, I sustained a debilitating injury and was met with a lack of empathy and manipulation from a nasty co-worker that tried to call me off of my doctor's note. Dealing with him triggered buried memories of other toxic workplaces, including the environment I worked in with Kevin, and finally pushed me to write this book.

My goal is to provide encouragement, insight, and strategies for coping and survival, as well as guidance for effectively quitting and moving on if you need to. I hope that my stories and advice will help you find peace and rise above your own workplace challenges. This book is for all those who have been affected by toxic workplaces, and just know that you don't have to end it all if you cannot handle work.

If you are feeling overwhelmed and work is becoming unbearable, remember that there is always help available and you do not have to end your life. Please reach out to someone you trust, or use one of the suicide resources below for support and guidance to get through your difficult time.

- Suicide & Crisis Lifeline: Dial 988 or 800-273-TALK (8255)
- Send a text: 838255
- For veterans: https://www.veteranscrisisline.net/get-help-now/chat/

Introduction

When a workplace becomes toxic, its poison spreads beyond its walls and into the lives of its workers and their families. –**Gary Chapman**

I t's Monday morning–again–already! I shuffle through the double doors and past the security guard as I flash my badge for him to see. *Yes, I work here. Unfortunately.*

The atmosphere shifts. It's a bit warmer as I make my way into the room full of cubicles, towards the one with my name on it. The sounds of keyboards clacking, fingers tapping, and phones ringing create a mild buzz in the office today. It's busy, as usual on a Monday. I would love to be in the moment, capable of enjoying the workday ahead of me, with confidence that what I am doing is important and is making some sort of difference somewhere.

But instead, anxiety begins to settle in. I spent all weekend working on the last-minute assignment my boss gave me before leaving Friday, and I wasn't able to spend the time I wanted with my children. At the slightest approach, question, or desire to share some wild story with me, my finger raised before my eyes ever did, pointing in the direction of their father.

Now, they're away at school, and I'm here, and I miss them so much that dread has fallen over me. I wish I would've asked my boss if the assignment could wait until today.

Then again, I already have a full stack of paperwork to go through that I have yet to make a dent in. Oh, how nice it would be to make it to my desk and see that someone was kind enough to help with my workload, *and–nope! Still here. I'm exhausted!* But this work has to get done and apparently there's no one else to do it but me. I would be glad when they get me some dependable help around here. The last girl never showed up for work, and when she did, she sat around on her phone all day. At least I could ask her to do something and she would–now, I have no one to even ask for help.

I thought this job would be different, but it turns out it's worse than my last one. Is there any hope of finding a job I can make into a career that doesn't require me to overextend myself in order to progress to the next level? Or does that not require me to choose between my family, a means of support for them, and my passions? This just can't be life. There has to be another way.

Maybe this story resonates with you. Maybe the character sounds like the voice in your head, or the circumstances they're facing reminds you of a similar time in your life. Does your life seem to revolve around a company that doesn't appreciate you? Do you feel like you're making no real impact—at least not how you'd hoped to? Is your world outside of those office walls caving in because of it?

If so, you're not alone. Hopefully, with a little Tender Loving Care (TLC), you'll learn how to begin taking better care of yourself and breaking free from toxic workplaces; so that you can find peace, both in and outside of the workplace, and enjoy what you do, all while making the money you deserve.

Toxic workplaces take many forms, but there is hope for you yet; you can overcome toxic work environments and the people that make them toxic. It all starts with you.

Take some time to think about what you want, who you are, who you want to be, and the impact you desire to make in your personal and professional life. The goal would be to find ways to make everything work together for your good and the good of everyone else around you, without compromising your soul.

Maybe you know what you want, and maybe you don't. All you know is that it is about time you UNCRUSH your soul and live again!

You have come to the right place. Here you will learn the skills you need to care for yourself in a way that allows you to extend that same care to others through your passion, job, and personal or professional relationships. You will learn how to impact your environment in a positive way instead of allowing the negativity to take a toll on you. You will learn how to be aware yet untouched while working towards your desired end and fighting for your rights, and the rights of those like you, in the workplace. You'll learn techniques to gain confidence in who you are and what you bring to the table, inside and outside of the workplace. Ultimately, you will learn how to cleanse your soul so that all of this, and then some, becomes possible for you.

The knowledge presented to you in this book took years of trial, error, and soul-crushing experiences, even a death, to acquire and apply. This is a process, but your being here indicates that you are ready to go through it. Kudos to you! Be encouraged that you may endure trial and error as well and that it is not a sign of weakness or a reason to give up. You've set a goal, and you should feel proud that you are determined to reach it, especially knowing that you are not the only person who has been, or is, where you are right now. It's time to begin the journey of uncrushing your soul. It's time to live again.

CHAPTER ONE

THE REAL COST OF A TOXIC WORKPLACE

When you envision a toxic work environment, what do you see? Is it a place where sexual innuendos and advances are the norm? Do you envision discriminatory behavior? A workplace where women are paid significantly lower rates than men, even though they may have more skill and experience under their belt? What about a workplace that promotes the tenure worker instead of the skilled worker because that's just policy? Does an environment where gossiping and slacking off is the norm come to mind?

While all of these are perfectly good examples of toxic work environments or contributors of toxic work culture, workplace toxicity can go far beyond these.

What is Workplace Toxicity?

A toxic work environment brings about challenges to progression, either by the company culture, co-workers, or even supervisors.

Virginia K. Billie created a chart that describes what a healthy environment looks like, it includes (Stojanovic, 2022):

1. Clear goals on a company-wide and personal level for each employee.

2. That attitudes, beliefs, and values are taken into consideration by employees, managers, and the organization.

3. Clear, concise, and open communication where feelings are allowed to be expressed and discussed openly.

4. That conflicts are resolved in a timely manner and are not pushed aside.

Simply put, everyone's time, differing backgrounds, and what they bring to the table as individuals must be valued, emphasized, and leveraged to not only grow the company but also to promote the growth of each person in all aspects of their lives.

Healthy work environments have all of these things and more. They openly communicate the goals and expectations from the beginning and uphold those goals and expectations throughout. A toxic work environment has the opposite qualities of those listed above.

There are some jobs that will communicate what they are looking for in prospective employees and what they have to offer in return, only for you to find out that their company culture is untrue to its word. In cases like you, you think you're getting yourself into a great situation, only to realize later down the road that you've been misled.

You start to realize that there is no effective communication between employees, there is an outrageous amount of gossiping going on, your boss has some narcissistic tendencies, and you don't want to work with anyone because you can't trust them. If this sounds like your workplace, then, unfortunately, you've found yourself in the midst of toxicity.

The Prevalence of Workplace Toxicity

Office toxicity is on the rise, and it is a very serious problem. You might chalk it up to, "I just need to change jobs," but the truth is, you may be just as likely to run into the same problems elsewhere, if not worse. When everyone isn't working toward a positive and healthy work environment, toxicity can be the result. Though change starts at the head, it is a team effort to make it work.

As reported in 2021, over half of the US labor force is made up of women. Yet it is also reported that women make significantly less than men in the same position, with the same amount of experience and skills. Women are just as vital to the progression of a company but are treated as though their work is less valuable than that of their male counterparts. Women are desiring recognition for their hard work and have begun to demand it. When a company runs into these kinds of issues in the workplace, they are bound to experience some blowback.

The toll this can have on working women is mental, emotional, and financial. Equality in the workplace would provide better opportunities for women, and men alike, to progress based on their work ethic, education, and skill rather than their gender or tenure alone. But this factor has yet to be mastered, even in today's workforce.

Alongside inequality in the workplace, people are starting to feel less engaged. Employees don't feel connected with their co-workers, and managers don't know how to get through to their employees; the company then takes a hit because of it.

In the era of COVID-19, many employees have taken their work home with them instead of working out of the office building. Although remote work has given employees the flexibility they desire, it has created a larger disconnect for some. Not to mention, it has allowed some of the workplace toxicity to follow employees home.

It used to be that, at least at the end of the night, employees could leave work and all of its drama behind, getting the chance to reset at home. That has become a harder task with remote work, as the confines of work walls are also home limits, and when you clock out, any negativity may linger in the environment. Not to mention, communicating with your supervisor is harder since you can never get a timely response via email. It's not like you can go up to them and talk to them when you see them because you don't get the chance to. The face-to-face interaction that benefited so many employees is no more. You were happy at first about being able to work at home, but you're now trapped by the demands of balancing work without any real guidance at home.

Employees are unhappy in their work which leads to depression and anxiety, which, in turn, can lead to physical illness. I was there and know this first-hand. My blood pressure nearly doubled when I was dealing with a very toxic situation, and I was so angry I failed to take care of myself, and my health suffered.

When you're not taking care of yourself mentally and emotionally, it becomes hard to take care of yourself physically. It is reported that America's health problems have cost employers a whopping $1.8 trillion annually. (54 Workplace Statistics–What Has Changed in 2021? 2021). Employers are also taking a hit in their employee retention rates. Some companies are extremely understaffed due to the toxic work culture, regardless of pay. When employees cannot be happy with the work they do in the environment they do it in, it makes them unmotivated and will eventually push them away from the workplace altogether.

The Negative Outcomes of Toxic Work Environments

Most people want to be recognized for their hard work. They want accolades, rewards, and even raises. When superiors overlook employees' strengths and acknowledge them, it could lead to negative feelings.

One of the main keys to making sure a work environment remains positive is to allow everyone to feel heard and seen for who they are, what they bring to the table, and the benefits their authenticity brings to the company. Sometimes differing backgrounds, personalities, opinions, and roles can lead to conflicts in the workplace. If conflicts remain unresolved for too long, they can lead to larger issues that negatively impact the company. Statistics show that "27% of employees involved in workplace conflict experience personal attacks, and about 25% either call in or skip work altogether" (54 Workplace Statistics–What Has Changed in 2021? 2021).

Conflicts in the workplace can include a number of things, such as discrimination based on age, gender, and race, gossip, harassment, devaluation, going unheard, misuse and abuse of power, and an all-around inconsideration and disrespect for someone's personal boundaries.

Employees who have to deal with these things in the workplace will become unmotivated, start to hate their job, or, in extreme cases, be afraid to show up to work. They may even open lawsuits against the company or complaints against the individuals who are causing the conflicts, especially those sitting in leadership positions. When these things begin to happen, an organization's reputation and business could be affected. People may not want to work for them or with them anymore. Employee resignation also means that those who choose to stay have to take on extra work to fulfill workflow requirements. Everyone is impacted when the work environment is toxic.

Toxicity in the Workplace and the Great Resignation

The Great Resignation, a term coined by economist Andrew McAfee, refers to the mass exit of employees from traditional jobs, particularly in the wake of the COVID-19 pandemic. This phenomenon has significantly impacted the job market, and it is essential to understand the causes and consequences of this trend.

One of the main drivers of this trend is the toxic work environment, where employees face burnout, long hours, office politics, lack of appreciation, and a sense of disillusionment. I might even be considered part of this mass exodus, pre-COVID when I was able to escape an extremely toxic job.

The COVID-19 pandemic has only amplified these feelings, as many workers have had to juggle work with homeschooling and other responsibilities. As a result, employees are choosing to leave their traditional jobs and seek more flexible and autonomous work arrangements, such as remote or freelance work. The Great Resignation had a significant impact on the job market, leading to increased competition for remote and gig work, decreased job security and wages for many workers, and companies struggling to fill open positions. It's crucial for companies to address the root causes of this trend and create a more supportive and flexible work environment to retain their employees and adapt to the changing needs of the workforce.

The Great Resignation also has implications for the future of work, as more and more employees are seeking better work-life balance and flexibility in their jobs. Companies that fail to adapt to this new reality risk losing valuable talent and struggling to attract new hires. Additionally, the trend towards remote work and the gig economy has highlighted the need for better support and resources for remote and freelance workers. This may include providing access to benefits, training and development opportunities, and tools to facilitate collaboration and communication.

Great Resignation is a complex phenomenon that is driven by a combination of factors, including the shift towards remote work, the rise of the gig economy, and most importantly, toxic work environment and employee dissatisfaction. To mitigate the negative effects of this trend, companies must take steps to address the underlying causes of employee dissatisfaction and create a more supportive and flexible work environment. This will not only help retain current employees but also attract new talent, and ultimately lead to a more productive and successful workforce.

Diversity, equity, inclusion, respect, and ethical behavior all seem to be things that drive workers to apply to, and remain with, a company (Hastwell, 2022). Without these things, regardless of the pay and popularity of a company, employees simply will not stay.

Do you know anyone who may have experienced a situation similar to this? Giving their all to a company, only to be unappreciated or discriminated against in return. This kind of inequality and harassment in the workplace may affect not only employees at work but outside of the workplace as well.

The Rise of Workplace Stress and Your Health

Movies and television shows tend to shine a light on traumatic experiences for women. They develop Post Traumatic Stress Disorder (PTSD) or other mental health issues of some sort. Then, you get to see how much she wants to move forward in health and freedom, but she just isn't able to because her fear cripples her. She is even afraid to speak up against her oppressor.

As a survivor of domestic violence and multiple near-death experiences, that was me 20+ years ago. After surviving those nasty things, over the years I began noticing this same cycle of abuse happening again and again in various work environments I was a part of.

The first one was many years ago, while I was still with my ex-husband/abuser and in my first job out of college. My ex would constantly call me at the office just to make sure I was there. One day I could not answer since I was in a meeting (this was before cell phones). He stomped into my office, started yelling at me in front of everyone, then punched the wall. Everybody was floored and could not believe what was happening. He was asked to leave, then I was called straight into my boss' office. Instead of asking me if I was alright (as one of my co-workers did), I got yelled at and reprimanded for my ex's actions. As if I could control that sociopath's actions, the boss told me that if he ever came back into the office again, I would be immediately fired. That action right there showed his poor leadership style and absolute lack of concern for one of his employees.

With that incident and more, I can say that this boss was the worst I ever had. To all of us new college graduates, he smugly offered an extremely low salary since "this is the best and largest agency in the state." We all bought into the allure of that selling point. All of us took the low salary and believed we were stuck there if we wanted to stay in the industry, despite the fact that all the workers at the coffee shop downstairs made more money than us.

I was expected to work 60-80+ hours a week while working long events with my clients almost every weekend, with no compensation days or overtime pay. The boss had no regard for personal or family time off and would laugh in our faces if any of us dared to ask for a comp day for working over the weekend. On top of that, we experienced his nepotism as he hired his sister-in-law to be a senior executive in the company. As she acted as an extension of the boss, she loved to yell at my co-workers and me as much as he did.

Experiencing all this as my 21-year-old self, the future looked pretty grim, which is completely opposite of how anyone should feel at that age. I eventually ended up getting a bleeding stomach ulcer from all the stress of that place, and that's on top of the bodily injuries I sustained from my ex's violence. I was facing a double whammy and needed to escape both situations.

Shortly after the wall-punching incident, I put in my two weeks' notice. I had no idea where I was going to go, and I did not care. I just wanted to be anywhere but there. I had absolutely no trust in that boss or the company as a whole. Since I had a difficult time letting go of the selling point that they were "the best and largest agency in the state," I felt trapped there. I finally came to the realization that the agency did not even matter, and at the end of the day, nobody truly cared about the company except for the handful of people running it. Once I truly grasped that concept, I knew my gut feeling was correct - the boss and company's values did not align with my own, and I effortlessly walked away and did not look back.

For me, this job was just the beginning of a string of toxic workplaces to come, and where I developed my work PTSD. Since I had no trust or respect for this boss, I also subconsciously expected a nasty boss with every future job.

When this type of workplace toxicity is accepted, workplace stress can become the result. Other stress in the workplace can come from things such as: "noise, poor lighting, poor office or work layout, ergonomic factors, high job demands, inflexible working hours, poor job control, poor work design and structure, bullying, harassment, and job insecurity." (Corporate Wellness Magazine, 2022). That's only to name a few. There are many reasons employees may experience stress in the workplace.

I have also seen work PTSD develop in my male counterparts, not just the females. One of them got very high blood pressure, and his numbers were off the charts. He was at high risk for a heart attack and stroke . . . all because of one toxic person. This co-worker was poison to our entire team and eventually caused a mass exodus since the leadership did nothing about him. Also, my blood pressure doubled, and I realized it was not worth my health or my sanity to stay and deal with the drama.

Workplace stress and health is a critical issue that affects all employees, regardless of gender. Men can be just as susceptible to the negative effects of toxic work environments as women. In fact, research has shown that men are at a higher risk of developing heart disease, the leading cause of death in men, as a result of workplace stress. Moreover, men can also develop PTSD as a result of their work environment.

One of the main sources of stress for men in the workplace is the pressure to be the primary breadwinner for their families. This pressure can lead to long hours, an excessive workload, and a lack of work-life balance. In addition, men may feel a sense of shame or stigma when they are unable to meet these expectations, which can further exacerbate their stress levels.

Furthermore, working in high-risk or high-stress fields, such as emergency services or the military, can lead to the development of PTSD symptoms, such as flashbacks, nightmares, and anxiety. Another source of stress for men in the workplace is the pressure to conform to traditional gender roles and expectations. Men may feel pressure to suppress their emotions, avoid vulnerability, and present a "tough" image to their colleagues. This can lead to feelings of isolation, loneliness, and a lack of support.

It's important for employers to recognize the unique stressors that men face in the workplace and to provide support and resources that can help them manage this stress. This can include providing flexible work arrangements, such as telecommuting or job sharing, to help men achieve a better work-life balance. Employers can also offer employee assistance programs, counseling services, and stress management training to help men cope with the demands of their jobs. Additionally, employers should provide resources and support for men who may be struggling with PTSD symptoms, such as therapy and time off.

It's also important for men to be able to speak openly about the stressors that they face in the workplace without fear of judgment. This can be facilitated by creating a culture of trust and open communication in the workplace. Men need to know that it's okay to ask for help and that seeking support is a sign of strength, not weakness.

Overall, it's crucial to recognize that workplace stress and health is an issue that affects all employees regardless of gender and that men are just as susceptible to the negative effects of toxic work environments as women. Employers and individuals need to work together to create a supportive and healthy work environment for all, including addressing the issue of workplace PTSD in men.

The most important thing to note is that workplace stress can have effects on employees' health and personal lives (regardless of gender) and in return, harm the company. Aristotle said it best, "Pleasure in the job puts perfection in the world." When employees are taken care of, companies reap the benefits.

CHAPTER TWO

HOW TO IDENTIFY TOXICITY IN YOUR WORKPLACE

"What do you know about making cable? You're just a stupid girl!" Yes, I was actually asked this question by my boss, as I had a pile of LC fiber cables on my desk that I just made.

I was the only female in the section, and our toxic boss was sexist and racist; it was obvious to everyone that I was his primary target. He would frequently make comments such as this in attempts to tear me down. He often went out of his way to imply that I was not a very good "technical person," and it was apparent he made these comments because of my gender (my male counterparts also noticed it). Being that I worked in a male-dominated technology field and military environment, this was fairly common in my experiences, and he was the extreme example.

Have you ever worked with that one person who just rubs you the wrong way? Unfortunately, I've had way too many of these. Perhaps they patronize you, overwork you, or have ridiculous expectations. What about those that can't wait to catch you at the coffee machine to mention the latest bit of juicy office gossip? It's easy to blame yourself and think, "I should put my foot down," or, "If only I could say no." While there are things you can do, you are not at fault for other people's behavior.

When Communication is the Problem

Communication is the key to success. Without communication, goals, expectations, objectives, boundaries, thoughts, feelings, emotions, and ideas cannot be shared properly or at all. Anyone can communicate. In fact, we are always communicating, whether it be verbally or nonverbally. However, communication is not always effective.

If your workplace has poor communication, you may notice that the giddy co-worker you once looked forward to seeing every day no longer shows up for work. You may get used to seeing the same co-workers hanging around the team leader's desk every morning, and those same people seem to get all of the special privileges. You'll find that the changes in policies and procedures within the company are unclear, as you always hear them through the grapevine and never directly from the horse's mouth.

Now, there are fewer team meetings. They used to be held once a week, but your team leader says that getting them approved with the new COVID-19 regulations is often a hassle and nearly impossible. So, you all have your team meetings once a month. Scheduling time with your team lead outside of that isn't an option, as they are usually busy with daily tasks and not around to schedule any one-on-one time. Whenever you have your meetings, the time is so limited that you cannot stay behind to steal a few minutes with them because you're being rushed to get back to work and meet productivity goals.

By now, your outlook on your job has changed. At first, you were excited; You felt as though you had this great opportunity. "Finally!" You thought, "A job that will allow me to grow, is very professional, and has great benefits. I can finally do the things I want to do, the things I've been dreaming of but just haven't had the funds to do."

However, since starting this job, nothing has been how you hoped or expected it to be. The things you were told during your interview process about the environment and company culture are not so much untrue as they are just not upheld. There is no real teamwork, nobody is on the same page, and because of this, your job has become harder to execute with efficiency. Poor communication does not only bring disunity in an organization, but it can also affect employee retention rates because no one really wants to work for a company that has no integrity and is disorganized. It makes their lives harder and more stressful.

Poor communication is no different in the workplace than it is in your personal relationships. For instance, if one of your personal relationships is suffering from a lack of active listening, is filled with reactions instead of responses, has constant misunderstandings, or one of you is refusing to speak to the other, there is going to be friction in the relationship, and it is going to suffer. You, or the other party, may decide it's not worth keeping the relationship. You've found that not being on the same page, being unheard, and the lack of boundaries–due to them being misunderstood, unheard, or miscommunicated altogether–is exhausting, and the relationship may come to an end. The same can be true for a company-employee relationship if communication is poor and causes many issues.

The Workplace Stuck in the Old Days

Sometimes a company can be unwilling to adjust to the current times. If a company is not evolving, there is very little chance of you doing so in its environment. It's like being in relationships that are stagnant because one or more parties are stuck in their ways; They do what they want and what they think is best instead of listening and taking advice to be able to serve the relationship well.

In 2016 a woman packed up and moved 45 minutes away from her home and two jobs, in which she made $22 an hour. She took a significant pay cut, making $9 an hour at her new job. However, what she discovered at this new job turned out to be more than she expected and worth every penny she left behind.

For the first time, she had a team lead who was invested just as much as she was invested in herself. It wasn't all about coming to work to make a dollar or pleasing her superiors; it was about doing the work well in an environment that served everybody.

The lead navigated leadership with ease, and integrity is what she lived by. She held herself to the standard of living honestly and kept that standard for her team and colleagues. She was good at being an open book, which was new to many of her team members. They weren't used to their superior showing up as a human who didn't micro-manage but instead walked alongside them. Someone who was completely unafraid to share the challenges she was facing to serve as motivation for her team, to let them know that they were not alone.

She held weekly team meetings where she would check in with her team. She would share team stats and create a plan to improve in areas where they needed improvement while also acknowledging how well they were already doing. She was great at leveraging their strengths instead of dwelling on their weakness and using each team member in areas where they would perform best.

She then moved on to opening the floor for them to voice any concerns or challenges they may have faced, whether in their personal or professional life. She would share words of encouragement and practice exercises that allowed her to connect with her team personally. She believed in treating her team as though they were a family because, in reality, they were a family away from their families. It kept them working together efficiently. As a result, her team had some of the highest statistics on the floor and were considered for promotions sooner than many of their counterparts.

This team lead was aware that leadership needs evolution and that the traditional way of leadership: distant, without any real connection, and robotic, with the only focus being what needs to get done each day, was not the best route to take and that people respond better to authenticity than they do to protocol.

It isn't always up to leadership in the workplace to ensure that things evolve as they should. Sometimes they aren't left with much room to do so. Some organizations do not allow their leadership the flexibility to be authentic with their teams, which stops team members from being authentic in return. A lot of what a team does, and does not do, falls back on the team's leadership, as they are supposed to be the overseers of their team's progression. This can put stress on leads that can then trickle down to the team. If a job is strict and inflexible about many things, it can cause employees' stress levels to get worse.

So, what happens when a job does not allow flexibility in schedules, processes, or procedures? When employees are overlooked and under-considered? When the single parent is ashamed of taking that time off from work for their child's activities or to accompany them to the doctor when they happen to get sick unexpectedly? Or when the promotions go to the worker who has been employed at the company the longest instead of the one with the most skills to fulfill the job needs? It can create an environment more prone to stagnation than growth for both the employees and the company.

And such situations happened to me repeatedly, leading me to seek other jobs over the years. My most recent experience happened in 2019 when I severely injured my knee from hiking. I tore four different areas in my knee from slipping on a muddy trail, and I was pretty much immobile. My doctor told me to stay completely off it and rest for at least two weeks while I was waiting for an MRI and a complete diagnosis. During this time, I could still telework while sitting on my couch with my laptop, and my boss seemingly understood the situation and authorized me to telework. A couple of days later, I received an email from my co-worker (not my boss) asking me to come in off my doctor's note. After I refused, I received a phone call from the boss asking me to come in . . . it was apparent that the co-worker manipulated our boss into forcing me into the office just because he "wanted me there."

Begrudgingly, I went into the office the next day, barely able to drive or walk. It took me about 20 minutes to hobble across the small parking lot and to my desk. When I got there, my co-worker nor my boss said anything to acknowledge me or the injury I sustained. It was just a regular day, with no big emergency as they made it out to be. On top of being very angry, I was in so much pain all day and couldn't wait for the day to end.

When I finally got home, I fell while getting out of my car and ended up re-tearing my knee. If they didn't call me into the office (for nothing), I would not have been driving, and I would not have fallen again! The intense anger I had at that moment was indescribable, and I knew I had to leave that organization. Previous to this, I was already looking for jobs because of my nasty co-worker, and that night I must have sent out at least 20 resumes. I was so desperate I was applying for all types of jobs, including ones that were out of my career field.

While reflecting on all this, I initially regretted not following my doctor's orders. Yes, I got hurt really badly again; however, mentally, this was a personal growth experience - if I didn't get so mad, I might still be stuck at that job today. The anger that incident generated inside me was my rocket fuel to get me the heck out of there.

The Adult Version of the School Playground

On the other side, when a company chooses not to monitor employee behavior at all, as opposed to monitoring it too closely, you might find yourself dealing with things that should not be acceptable in the workplace. This too can cause stress, disunity, disorganization, and all kinds of conflicts.

For example, suppose you are always needing to work harder because the company failed to hire dependable workers or enforce its attendance policy to challenge its employees to come to work when scheduled. In that case, you can find yourself burnt out and ready to call it quits. Now, not only does the company have a case of undependable workers, but it is failing to retain workers because of its unprofessionalism.

A company that does not enforce its policies opens doors for its employees to take full advantage of them. Employees choose to show up to work when they want or choose when they actually complete work when they're there. But you may find some other forms of unprofessional behavior as well, such as the employee who comes to work only to gossip. They have found their group of people to clique up with, and they are constantly taking up work hours spilling the latest tea or spreading rumors about others. Their priority isn't the company and its mission, but they have their own purposes for coming to the workplace. This kind of behavior could lead to bullying and harassment, which are unacceptable in the workplace. If not dealt with, or a non-tolerance policy is not enforced, a company could lose its employees.

Energy Vampires in Your Workplace

Another form of toxicity in the workplace is people, co-workers, and leadership, who drain you of your energy and make it hard to focus on your work. They just have all-around exhausting personalities and may not even know it. These intense personalities are referred to as energy vampires. For their own personal reasons, they feed off of the energy of others. Being the kind, caring, and compassionate hard worker that you are makes you a great target.

Some energy vampires are not intentionally exhausting. They may not know any better or realize that their behavior is harmful. That is why dealing with them in the workplace takes some intentionality, honesty, and bravery on your part.

There are different kinds of energy vampires. Knowing which one you are dealing with can make it easier to know how to be intentional when it comes to preserving your energy. You want to ensure you're using the right techniques for the right person.

There are three main types of energy vampires you may encounter in the workplace. They are *the melodramatic, the egomaniac,* and *the dependent* (Wilding, 2022).

The melodramatic is drawn to drama. You will find that they either overshare about their personal lives or are continually dishing out the latest tea about others. They can also be labeled as "the gossiper." This form of energy vampire has no concept of personal boundaries and may not really be aware that they are crossing them. Either way, their overextension of themselves can make anyone uncomfortable.

The egomaniac energy vampire has a sense of entitlement. Their world is all they care about. They may be obnoxiously negative or constantly in attack mode. They are usually mind manipulators. They may go the extra mile to make themselves look better than they are by down-talking others and praising themselves. Their end game makes others doubt themselves to get them to do what they want. These people are sometimes acting out of a need to fill a void within themselves, a place where they are not in assurance of themselves and don't want anyone to know it. So they portray themselves in a light that casts darkness on everyone else.

The dependent suffers the need to be validated often. They may have been under the influence of *the egomaniac* at one point and now doubt their capabilities as an individual. Their doubt in themselves is so strong that they shy away from thinking or acting authentically and as a result, become people pleasers. They want to keep those around them happy, and it often comes at the expense of themselves. Sometimes these folks doubt themselves so much it drives their anxiety through the roof and turn into spazzy messes that drive everyone around them nuts. Because of their doubt, they may constantly ask boatloads of questions before making any decision to make sure that they are making the right choice. In the workplace, this can be a hindrance because it slows down productivity for the whole team. This energy vampire is unintentionally extremely exhausting. They are well-meaning, pure in heart and deed, and easily imposed upon.

Unfortunately, I've had my share of all these, and there are different ways to handle working with each of these energy vampires in the workplace. The main thing to remember is to be firm, set your boundaries, and enforce them regularly. I will expand on this in later chapters.

When Your Career is Going Nowhere

For most, choosing a career is hard enough. You spend almost your whole life trying to find what piques your passions or makes you passionate. Then, when you find that thing, you have to decide where you can express that passion through your work. Some workplaces make this a hard task to accomplish. When you have to team up with unmotivated co-workers, sit under the authority of non-motivational leadership, or work within an organization that is not very organized, your passion can be stifled.

An environment full of unmotivated workers can make being driven feel like running around like a chicken with its head cut off. Your co-workers' slack will make you have to work harder on tasks that may either be outside of your job description or outside of your time constraints. You'll find yourself carrying the weight of others all the time, especially if you have unqualified, incompetent co-workers that do not know how to do their job and tries to fake it. Everyone needs a little help sometimes, but it becomes distracting and exhausting when it becomes a regular thing. Burnout and a loss of inspiration will be the results.

An overt amount of unmotivated workers has a root cause deeper than the workers themselves. It may fall under the category of the organization.

There is possibly something they are doing or some practice they have not yet adopted that would benefit their employees and make them more motivated to do their job.

Whatever the case, you will encounter stagnation when your team is not working as a team. No one wants to lead a life going nowhere, so if your job makes it easier for you to fail than to succeed, it may be time to make some adjustments.

Manipulation in the Workplace

Manipulation in the workplace can be hard to recognize. Sometimes your gut can tell you that you may be experiencing it, but then there are the factors that make you doubt whether your gut is being truthful. What if the one manipulating you is superior? Or a truly genuine person? What if you have a history of misjudging others based on distrust? What if you have a sweetheart that sees the best in people and tends to overlook the bad? You don't believe they could do that to you or anyone else because people are generally good, right? Whatever the case, manipulation in the workplace is real, and it happens all the time.

There are five main things to look for to help you discern manipulative behavior:

1. **Low Spirits/Vibes**: Something about being around this person saps your energy and makes you feel low. You are never happy around them, and it always feels off. If you feel this way, this is a sign for you to take a step back and evaluate why that may be

to pinpoint the manipulative behavior exactly, but the vibe you feel doesn't lie. Their presence shifts your atmosphere and can be either one of two people: you or them. If you can honestly look at yourself and say it is not you, you have your answer. As a new guy walked into our office, I instantly felt a shift in the room's energy. He didn't bother to shake my hand, as my arm was still extended, and he seemed very arrogant. I immediately knew that he was bad news. Although I never had to work directly with him, I hated seeing him since I would feel drained just being around him. He was the king manipulator as he convinced leadership that he was God's gift to the world. Later, he ended up being why multiple people left the organization. I wasn't surprised since I would only see a frown on his face, he was very gruff and rude, and to this day, he is the only person that has thrown a stack of papers at me during a meeting.

2. **Extreme Obligation**: If you feel an extreme sense of obligation to a person, and it makes you place your needs and desires on the back burner to fulfill them for fear of not pleasing that person, you could be getting manipulated. This is common if your boss lays guilt trips on you for supposed favors they did for you and expects you to drop everything for them - maybe for a raise, a day off, a promotion, etc. I saw this happen when one boss kept asking my co-worker to drive him to the airport on weekends and evenings for his personal trips. For some reason, he would only ask this one co-worker for rides and not anyone else. I suspect it might be because the boss appointed him as the team leader. The

boss attempted to lay guilt trips on him, but thankfully he never folded, stuck to his guns, and never drove him to the airport.

3. **Alter Ego**: If you start to alter who you are or how you act because who you are is not good enough to please your boss or colleagues, they may be manipulating you. You should be able to be around them without always having something negative to say or without it being an issue. Of course, those who can be trusted to hold you accountable should be honest with you constructively and challenge you to grow, but they will not try to control you. These people will not be okay with you changing to fit into a little box of theirs. They would encourage you to be authentic and perform your best in your role.

4. **Emotional Instability**: One minute, your boss is fine and calm, and the next, you don't know what's happening with him, and he's about to explode. You're afraid you might say or do something that sends him through the roof, so you always play it safe while constantly walking on eggshells. This kind of manipulation can be hard to spot. Still, I've seen this often with those I suspect have borderline personality disorder or are narcissists (mostly in the previously mentioned egomaniacs). Sometimes your manipulating boss could have a hard time dealing with his emotions. Instead of personally finding effective ways to deal with them, he projects his negative feelings onto everyone on the team and attempts to make them responsible for how he feels. You must keep the bigger picture in mind for your sanity when dealing with

these bosses. However, suppose you do not stand your ground with them. In that case, they will never understand the need to work towards a change in their behavior for a positive impact on the team.

5. **Feeling Devalued**: You are constantly trying to prove your worth to your boss or colleagues and doing the very best you can, but still, nothing you do or say is ever good enough for them. If you are experiencing this, it means you are already on their s-list, and they hate you. The boss I mentioned earlier with my cable story - this was him. He loved to put me down about everything, especially my "nonexistent technical skills." He would also insult me about non-work-related topics, such as the type of food I ate (he called it "weird Asian food") or how slow I ran my marathons (even though he was not even a runner, nor never ran a marathon in his life, and was overweight). My other co-workers noticed he would pick on me the most, and they thought it was because I was the only female on the team. It's as if his goal was to make my days as miserable as possible by trying to cut me down. Manipulators have ways of turning things back on you if confronted for their behavior. The term for it is "gaslighting." They want you to doubt that you are right about them, or anything for that matter, by making you feel crazy for acknowledging your suspicions. They do this because they want to be able to still use and abuse you for their benefit or, at the very least, feel good about themselves without having to change.

Whether in your personal or professional life, manipulation can take a heavy toll on you. It is important to take note of the deceitful behavior and end it as quickly and efficiently as possible. If not, you can lose yourself and find that your joy and peace have left you. At that point, you'll have to work even harder to get it back.

Signs Your Boss is Causing the Toxicity

More likely than not, bosses are the major manipulators in the workplace. To be oppressed by the one who makes sure you are paid, controls if you keep your job, and has the power to make good or bad referrals to any other job you may pursue in the future, can be terrifying. Because of this, they may be the last ones to be called out for their unacceptable behavior.

Have you ever had a boss where you just wondered, "How in the world did they get in their position of power? Who put them there and why? What leadership qualities did they show before to make them worthy of being anyone else's boss? Have they always been this obnoxious?" You probably had that one person (or many, like me) you had to work for who was impossible. They make your job harder for no other reason than that they can. I'm here to tell you that you should never have to deal with that again.

Now that you know what a toxic work environment can look like, it is time to do the work. First, look at yourself and ensure you are not displaying any of these toxic qualities in the workplace. If you are, acknowledge and deal with this behavior quickly because the change starts with you first. Then, evaluate your co-workers, superiors, and the organization you work for and determine if there are any toxic behaviors there. Do you notice any?

It's easy to say you will end toxic behavior, but it could be decades of habitual behavior that have become unconscious habits. So, rather than charging in like a bull in a china shop, you need to learn and apply the proper skills to handle each situation correctly. In the upcoming chapters, this is exactly what you'll learn to do, starting with learning to set healthy boundaries.

Chapter Three

Change Starts With You

I was the master of setting boundaries at home. Just raising an eyebrow was enough to let my kiddos know they were dancing on a dangerous line, and consequences would soon ensue. But as soon as I was at work, I lost touch with that boundary line. I had no idea about my boundaries or how to establish and enforce them. I knew that until I learned to set them, people would continue to take advantage of me.

Don't let your identity be defined by your job. When you meet someone for the first time, and they ask you what you do for a living - do you tell them what your job is, or do you tell them who you really are? In my experience, the majority of people will answer that question with what their job is, even if they are retired from it. It is worth asking yourself if that is truly what you want to be known as.

This used to be me, but over the years I have learned to separate my true identity from what I did at work, as work started to eat me alive. I have been in some places that were so disturbing that it affected my entire mood for days, weeks, and months on end, and I let it torment me at home too. I found myself angry all the time, and while I was at one place, my blood pressure doubled, I got migraine headaches every single day, and my muscles were constantly locked up. I should not have let it affect my health, but I did. It took years, but I learned that my job does not define me, and yours does not either, so don't let it!

Types of Boundaries Necessary at Work

Boundaries are a set of rules or moral standards you live by. They protect you from conflicts, miscommunications, and burnout, either in your personal or professional life.

Setting boundaries in the workplace can be challenging. You may not want to upset your boss or appear to be any less of a team player to your co-workers, but boundaries are pertinent to your health, happiness, and productivity. A lack of boundaries can leave you distracted and distorted. Let's look at some areas in which asserting boundaries is necessary.

1. **Physical**: This one may seem like a given and shouldn't have to be spoken about, but that is not always the case. You should never expect people to know what your physical boundaries are, as they can be different for different people. One person may naturally be more outgoing than another person. They may not have strict boundaries when it comes to things like needing some personal space to recuperate or get work done, but you do. And if you don't communicate that you need some space, you might have some

people who impede on your space. Physical boundaries are there to help you take care of your body and personal space.

2. **Emotional and Intellectual**: To set boundaries emotionally and intellectually, you have to have a solid connection with yourself. There has to be a willingness to have your own thoughts, opinions, and ideas. You must also provide others the space and grace to do the same. Setting boundaries in this area is not only meant to be beneficial to you but to others as well. When you have boundaries for others not to cross, you tend not to cross those boundaries for them, either. This is why the connection with yourself is important. When you are connected to yourself and better able to understand yourself, you can extend that same understanding to others. When you can understand others, you can communicate with them more efficiently because you can communicate with them from their level of understanding. Setting emotional and intellectual boundaries not only keeps others from being toxic toward you, but it also keeps you from being toxic toward others. As mentioned before, change starts with you.

3. **Priority and Workload**: You may be tempted to blow this one off as being not as important or beneficial to you if you are an employee who's not in a leadership role, as this one may seem to benefit them more. But it will have great benefits for you as well. If you happen to be one of those people who are really good at your job and are always being asked to help with team tasks, you know that there are days when you just aren't feeling it. When adding

certain tasks to your schedule that could set you back in your own work or just exhaust you, it is appropriate to set the expectation that maybe your teammates can try getting it done on their own this time or kindly redirect them to someone else who may be willing to help out. Members of leadership, and those in the team, should practice openly communicating when their workload is full and set the expectation that a team works together to get tasks done. Setting these boundaries can reduce the chances of burnout and allow everyone to be able to show up and give their best each day. It just takes some team effort.

4. **Time**: Every minute spent is another minute gone, and you cannot get your time back. It is advisable to spend it wisely. Setting time boundaries can be the hardest thing to do because it requires self-discipline and respect from others, and you cannot make people respect you; you can only earn it. It's inevitable that schedules will be interrupted sometimes; things happen that are out of our control, of course. So when you have control over your time, take advantage of it. You have to say no to some of the things that are claiming your time and are counterproductive. For example, you have a deadline a week from today, and you have it marked on your calendar. Each day you have a short-term goal to get a certain amount done by the end of the workday, starting today. You decide that you want to get to work an hour early and sit in the breakroom so you can have some quiet time to work on that project. Your co-worker notices you're in early and decides to come up to you and talk to you since they know you don't

have to be clocked in anytime soon. They're rambling about what happened in the office last night when you left, and, honestly, you don't care. You just want to be able to focus on what you came in early to do, but you don't know how to tell your co-worker without coming across as rude. However, if you do not communicate what you need, co-workers may never know when you need space to focus. Find ways to communicate what you need in a respectful way towards others so that they will understand, and that will produce the results you are aiming for. If you need to, have clear physical boundaries, such as earphones in your ear, sit away from everyone in a full room, or sit in a private room alone, etc. When you decide what you want your visual barrier to be, explain to others that it means you are taking the time for yourself and prefer no interruptions at those times.

5. **Communication**: Can you honestly say you leave work hoping your boss, or one of your employees, calls you? No, probably not. When you leave work, you want work to stay where it is, but sometimes things come up. Maybe a co-worker got sick and called in for their shift, now the job needs a cover person, or business is much busier than predicted, and the person in charge of the schedule did not assign enough workers, so your manager is asking people to stay overtime. These things happen. So how do you let your team know when you are available for communication and when you'd prefer to be undisturbed? Explain to your superior before leaving work if you'll be available if they need you. If not, tell them, "Hey, tonight is family night. I prefer not to be contact-

ed regarding any work crisis." Place your phone on *do not disturb* when you get home, and require people to leave messages if they want to reach you. Log out of your email during your off time and tell people you are not online. With all of these things, find ways to set expectations that you will reach back out when you are available. Set hours that you are available for communication and hours where you will be disconnecting from any modes of communication. Share those hours with those you work with so that they don't expect you to get back to them immediately or feel the need to keep trying to reach you.

Boundaries are pertinent to your health, and they show people how to treat you. When you don't set boundaries, you are giving others permission to treat you as they see fit, and that may not always be in ways that you agree with. Without boundaries, you can find yourself stretched thin, allowing toxicity in. Be honest about who you are and your limits, especially when it comes to work. Set boundaries early on and openly share them with your hiring team, superiors, and co-workers so that you have a chance to create an environment conducive to your needs. If people at work cannot respect your boundaries, it's okay. That job just might not be the one for you, and there will be better ones. There are jobs out there that will not make you compromise yourself and your values to have them. The choice is always yours in the end - you are the captain of your own ship. My big lesson learned is the instance mentioned previously about my knee injury. If I held my boundary by following my doctor's orders, I would not have compromised my health and re-injured my knee.

Do You Know Your Workplace Expectations?

Along with setting expectations in your workplace, there are things that will be expected of you. These expectations should be communicated to you from the beginning, giving you the chance to decide if you can accept the terms and conditions of the job or not. Sometimes you might find that the expectations are laid out in the job description or on the application and may be reiterated to you during the interviewing and hiring process. Some expectations that may be laid out in the job description would be physical demands, the type of environment you'll be expected to work in, duties, requirements, and pay.

Physical demands let you know if you will be sitting or standing for long periods of time, if you'll be lifting heavy objects on any given day, and require you to be able to make it to work on time when scheduled, with or without accommodations.

Environmental expectations may let you know if the work is fast-paced or if the environment is family-friendly. With the changes from COVID-19, these expectations may include whether or not your work can be done remotely or if you have to wear a mask or be vaccinated to enter the building.

Some requirements may be needing a high school diploma, a college degree, or a certain degree in a specific field. They'll let you know if you have to have your own equipment when working from home and what that equipment would need to be.

Duties would be laid out in the description and in your conditional offer letter, letting you know what the scope of your work is. If the duties listed are vague, ask questions. Make sure you have a complete understanding of what will be required of you. Your pay is usually contingent upon the duties laid out to you, if you are being asked to do more than what is within your scope of duties, you are allowed to ask for more pay to compensate for it.

Always read over any contracts you are asked to sign before signing them. A man walked into a temp service near his home, looking for work once. He was told this place was hiring on the spot, and the position they were hiring part-time workers for paid $23 per hour. He would be working three days a week, 10-hour shifts each day, and this was okay with him. He had his off days with his family, and he would be earning an income as if he was working full-time.

Then, suddenly his checks started getting lower and lower, but he was putting in all of his hours. Confused, he had to call the temp service where he was hired and inquire about it. He was told that he signed some papers that gave an insurance company permission to deduct money from his weekly check. He was unaware of what was in the paperwork he signed because he paid no attention to it. Eager to start work, he signed what was placed before him and asked no questions. Apparently, it was not explained to him either. He had to jump through hoops from there to get the insurance deductibles removed from his checks.

Things like this are great reasons to pay close attention to the paperwork you sign, ask questions - know what you want, and set expectations. If you are not setting expectations, you could be agreeing to do a job that will not suit you. If you don't ask questions, you may find that what is expected of you is not conducive to your growth and health. Or, like the man who was eager to have work, you may be signing off on something that will cause a hit to your finances later. It's best to be aware and stay updated.

How to Set Your Workplace Boundaries

As discussed earlier, there are some main areas to assert your boundaries in the workplace. Let's now have a look at ways to set those boundaries.

Setting boundaries requires that you first know what they are. "Your boundaries will stem from your values and life priorities." (Career Contessa, 2022). It begins in your personal life and should extend to your professional life. What matters to you will show in the boundaries you choose to set for yourself and for others. As previously mentioned, setting boundaries for yourself is just as important as setting boundaries for others because it will likely be your guide in setting boundaries for others. You must know what works best for you, what you do and do not want, and what you will and will not accept, even from yourself. Know your limits and embrace them. It's that inner voice reminding you of who you are.

While you shouldn't spend so much time on your feelings or allow them to make decisions for you, it is still healthy to acknowledge them. Feelings can reveal secret things that may not be apparent at the surface. Even if you don't completely understand them right away, pay attention to them.

Aside from knowing your limits, and acknowledging how things make you feel, give yourself permission to have these feelings and set limitations for yourself and for others. No one else is going to give you permission to be authentically you. It is a decision that you will have to make on your own. Sometimes, it could come at the cost of the life, job, or relationship you thought you wanted. However, if things are not aligning with who you are, you should not have to change yourself to fit in or accept them. Not to say don't challenge yourself, but ultimately what is for you will gravitate towards you when you are being authentic. You may find that what you originally wanted is not what you want at all, and what you find while standing on who you are is what you actually need. So be clear about what you stand for. Remember this nugget if setting your boundaries results in you needing to step out on faith - *never compromise your soul.*

Having a system is also important when setting boundaries. In other words, you must have discipline. If you're expecting others to take your boundaries seriously, you must take them seriously. Make sure that your system is beneficial to you and to others. Setting boundaries in the workplace is not to be self-centered but to make everyone's work a little less stressful. You still want to be a team player. Systems help things to run smoothly and allow any detours to be navigated with ease.

Remember to be transparent about your boundaries. However, if being too personal with your co-workers makes you uncomfortable or could potentially cause conflicts in the future, keep your work relationships professional. Disclose minimal information about your personal life. Know the difference between your friends and associates, compartmentalize wisely, and keep things on as much of a need-to-know basis as necessary.

Don't forget, in all of your boundary settings, to establish that invisible line for yourself. Do not be afraid to say "No." Take some time off from work, allow yourself some me-time, be off-limits (if you must be), and mentally prepare! Prepare yourself for those boundary-breaking co-workers and bosses! Be ready and willing to handle, with care and professionalism, of course, those who refuse to respect the boundaries you have put in place because you will indeed encounter them.

Expressing Your Boundaries the Effective Way

Do you remember how I said effective communication is the key to success? Communicating your boundaries is the most effective when it is simply put. Be specific and to the point, do not elaborate too much or try to justify your boundary, and never apologize for your boundaries (Block, 2021).

Recognize what your boundaries are and why they are there. Being honest with yourself first makes it easier to be honest with others. It can be a scary thing to face yourself. It's easy to hide behind a mask when you want to please others, but choosing YOU means dropping the mask.

You do not have to explain to others why you have a boundary. Leave it on the need-to-know. All they really need to know is that you have this boundary and that you expect them to respect it. If they cannot respect it, you must choose what to do from there.

Just be sure that you are clearly stating what your boundaries are. If you are not clearly stating your boundaries, you may leave some room for confusion, and, even worse, people may not treat you the way you expect them to. Be clear about what you want and set expectations, but don't be a ruling machine. Setting boundaries should not make you a control freak. Yes, you should be in control of your life, but you cannot control others. As you expect others to give you the space to be who you are, you have to find the common ground to reciprocate that energy.

Remember to start small, and try not to change too many things at once. There's no pressure to hurry this process. Pace yourself by using the three communicative steps to expressing boundaries – acknowledge, state the boundary, and articulate expectations – you will be able to get your point across well each time.

What to Do When Your Boundaries Are Crossed

It would be nice to believe that setting boundaries will be the answer to all of your problems in the workplace and that as long as you are communicating effectively and clearly expressing yourself in a professional and respectful manner, everyone will get on board. But unfortunately, that is not always the case. You're bound to run into some people who do not understand your boundaries and their importance or those who simply just do not care. Not everyone is going to respond the way you would like them to when it comes to setting boundaries in the workplace. If you're dealing with someone who does not respect your boundaries, you may need to take some steps to show them how serious you are.

If a co-worker is not respecting your boundaries, try reiterating and rein-forcing your boundary at the very moment they are crossing it. Give them a few chances to get it right, as adjusting takes a little longer for some than others. Three chances are a fair amount. If, after the third time, you have to remind them, and they are not actually putting in the work to change their behavior and respect your boundary, it may be time to take your concern to someone who has a little more power to yield some results.

No one wants conflict in the workplace. It makes things stressful, de-teriorates your focus, and, sometimes, pushes you to feel like the job is not worth it. You have the right to be respected. Go to your immediate supervisor if the co-worker continues their behavior. They should schedule a sit down with the two of you to discuss ways to deal with and overcome the issue so that you may continue to work together.

If the sit-down does not work and your co-worker continues their behav-ior, or the behavior worsens as a form of retaliation for you talking to your supervisor, it may be time to take it to someone higher than your supervisor. Some jobs have an open-door policy. If your organization is not living up to its stated policy, or if what your co-worker is doing is not enough for them to have a consequence, you may decide that someone outside of your organization is the route that you want to take.

I found myself in this situation multiple times. However, I only once filed a complaint to the higher powers when one particular co-worker caused a mass exodus. My boss knew this co-worker was messed up and was causing a huge disturbance and unbalance to the team, as everyone wanted him gone. He did nothing about it, and after nearly two years of dealing with him, I could not stomach it anymore and decided to leave. On my way out, I filed a joint complaint with other co-workers that included just about everything you can think of, from creating a hostile environment, harassment, gender and age discrimination, bullying, favoritism, and more. Dealing with him was just not worth my health or my sanity. Sadly, the leadership there did not do anything about him despite having multiple complaints/testimonies stating the exact same thing.

If you find that your workdays become more about you fighting for your right, as I mentioned above, in order to have boundaries and be treated with respect, it is up to you to decide if it is something you can handle moving forward and if you're willing to keep up the fight or not. The co-worker I mentioned previously had no respect for my boundaries, so it was my choice to leave. While it will be a challenge, setting boundaries in your workplace should not be a hassle. Knowing what is expected of you by your employer from the beginning is going to help understand why your co-worker is not respecting your boundaries. You cannot control if your organization will hold each employee accountable, but you can take steps to make sure that they know you are serious about your expectations of them and your co-workers.

Setting boundaries with co-workers and bosses alike requires excellent management of your emotions. You may entertain the idea of talking to a therapist in this regard. You can practice ways to share your discomforts and frustrations clearly and in a professional way. You can learn how not to allow the insignificant actions of others to control who you will be and how you will show up in the workplace. You can have control over your emotions if nothing else.

Chapter Four

The Crucial Role of Emotional Intelligence in the Workplace

Don't you just love that boss that is so smart? They always have these amazing ideas, and every time you look up, they add more letters to their name. Yet, whenever you ask for time off to pick your sick kid up, they look at you as if you asked them the meaning of life. Intellect can only get you so far. Without the ability to relate to people and their emotions, you will never foster a positive environment.

Emotional intelligence, often referred to as emotional quotient (EQ), is the ability to recognize and properly express emotions. (Cherry, 2020). Emotions can run high, especially when you are triggered. For this reason, it is important to know what your triggers are, why you are triggered, and to have a plan to manage any emotions that may stem from your triggers. A trigger is anything that makes you emotional. When you know what triggers you and have a plan to manage the emotions that arise properly, it can keep you from acting in inappropriate ways in your personal life and in the workplace.

Taking the time to understand your emotions and why you have them can help you better understand and relate to others when they feel triggered and emotional. When you can connect with others on a deeper level, you will find that your relationships benefit greatly. The positive change you seek will always start with yourself, so in this chapter, we will discover ways to evaluate yourself and how you can contribute to a positive work environment.

Becoming emotionally intelligent can take some practice and skill setting. We are taught emotional skills from childhood. Environments, backgrounds, beliefs, and experiences are among some of the things that can shape emotional skills. If you grow up in a household where effective communication is null and void, you may not grow up to become the best communicator. If you're used to hearing yelling and seeing outbursts when emotions are high, you will probably think this is the right way to handle high emotions. Even if you know this to be the wrong way to handle your emotions, unlearning the behavior can be a challenge. You may have been bashed for speaking up for yourself, so now you hold everything in and allow things that don't make you feel very well. You may handle your emotions by retreating from everyone for long periods of time without any explanation. There is hope for you yet. You can choose to learn emotion management skills. These skills will come in handy and help you to succeed in all areas of your life.

The Role of Emotional Intelligence in the Workplace

Attitude means a lot. Perspective is everything. How you view and respond to things will be the determining factor in your growth and progress in life. In the workplace, checking your attitude and choosing to evaluate the way you view things can be life-changing in your work environment. Remember that everyone comes from different backgrounds, is raised differently, has different views, values, and beliefs, and goes about life differently. Sometimes you will have to agree to disagree. Most times, you can challenge yourself to learn something new, expand your view, and live and work outside of the box.

Most workplaces in the year 2022 are diverse. You will work with all kinds of people from all over the globe. If you lack emotional intelligence, you could jeopardize important work relationships and make work awkward. Having emotional intelligence will be your guide in dealing with others effectively, no matter how different you are from each other. It not only makes you more competent but is also proven to be a stress reliever in the workplace. It is exhausting to have your guard up at all times because of emotions. When you expand your point of view, you may preserve yourself from taking things offensively when they were not meant to be.

So, how can you tell if you have a low EQ? Well, there are some telltale signs that a person has low emotional intelligence and if you are one of those people, you have to be open to learning and growing. Also, if you spot these people in your workplace, you have to have the skill to engage and work with them. Low emotional intelligence can have negative impacts on your work, the success of those around you, as well as the company or organization itself. Someone with low emotional intelligence may not respond well to co-workers and leadership, they might also respond horribly to customers, and this could cause horrible employee retention rates as well as a loss in profits for the company. Organizations would benefit from having emotion management training for employees and providing resources for employees to seek professional assistance outside of work.

Spotting the Emotionally Unintelligent

People with low emotional intelligence are usually self-centered; They struggle to acknowledge anyone or anything outside themselves. The effect of this self-centeredness creates a distance, and even failure, in relationships. You might find that people who struggle to manage their emotions healthily have very few personal relationships and struggle with effective communication and relationship-building in the workplace.

When a person is self-centered, they may lack empathy for others and not understand the importance of viewing things from another's perspective. What matters to them is having their way; There isn't any middle ground they'll be willing to meet you on. They always want to be the most important in the room and can't acknowledge others' efforts or congratulate their successes. You may find them making subtle snarky comments at every turn. Being positive about anything can be a challenge for these people.

People with low emotional intelligence may also have difficulty adapting to change or coping with stress. They may be controlling, and when they find that the control is out of their hands, it may send them into depression or cause them to have emotional outbursts. Constant emotional outbursts signal a person who does not recognize, acknowledge, and manage feelings well. Sometimes, they may place responsibility on others to manage their emotions, getting upset when others are not walking on eggshells around them and bending to their every demand. What is happening inside of them could be misunderstood, and in return, they lash out at others because they have not developed the skills to properly express what is happening.

When people are disconnected from themselves in such a way, effectively connecting with others is impossible. How can you understand someone else when you don't understand yourself? Whatever relationship you hold with yourself, you will hold with those around you. If you blame yourself for things unnecessarily, it may translate into blaming others for everything because you don't like to view yourself as the problem. Looking in the mirror can be a hard thing to do, but that is exactly what we are going to do later on when we discuss how to improve emotional intelligence.

Checking in With Your Emotional Intelligence

Do you run at the sight of stressful situations? Does change scare you so much that you do everything in your power to prevent it from happening? When you're down, do you look to substances for comfort, or do you have healthy things that you do to lift your spirits? Do you embrace your not-so-good, as well as your good emotions, or do you shun yourself and feel bad for having them? Do you have a good work-life balance?

The answers to these questions determine your level of EQ. A low EQ will result in less productive and less positive outcomes in your personal and professional life. For example, you encounter a snag in the road in your personal life that has affected your relationships, and instead of allowing the challenge to help you learn and grow, you allow it to push you towards discouragement. You become unmotivated in your personal and professional life and stop giving your best. The challenge seems too much to overcome, so you look to self-soothe with pity and maybe even substances. Stress management is a good indicator of EQ. If your ability to handle stress well is almost non-existent, it could be time to work towards developing some management skills for your emotions.

Maybe you have encountered an extremely traumatic event in your life that still triggers you at any moment. Traumatic events are inevitable in life and to know how long they will trigger you is nearly impossible. Some things you may never get over, but you can decide how you will choose to respond to those triggers. If your response to triggers is always dramatic and inappropriate, to the point where people tend to opt out of being around you or make subtle comments about your sanity, you may want to consider alternative and healthy ways to handle your triggers.

Sometimes a low EQ can be spotted by a simple inability to be emotionally close to others. If emotional situations make you uncomfortable and you try your hardest to avoid them, you may be a bit out of touch with your own emotions or have a hard time acknowledging and accepting them. An inability to be emotionally close to others can cause you to be insensitive toward feelings and emotions. It can make you distant and aloof, which isn't always a good thing as relationships help propel success and promote health.

So, how do you make changes to raise your EQ and connect with others on a deeper level to be more successful in your life? In the next section, you will learn some practical tips for bettering yourself, by connecting with yourself, understanding yourself, embracing yourself, and extending the care and attention that you give yourself to others so that you can make a positive impact on your environment. If you are not there yet, it is okay, the following tips will help you get there.

How to Improve Emotional Intelligence for Yourself and the Office

Whenever the goal is to make a change in the world around us, we must first start with ourselves. Whatever we want to see, we have to put out. As is the case, life is like a mirror; whatever is given to us is probably a reflection of what we have been given, and we may or may not recognize it.

A great start would be evaluating yourself. Are there any toxic behaviors mentioned in this book that you fit the description for? If so, how does it make you feel to know that you have been a toxic individual toward those around you? Evaluate and acknowledge these feelings and be brave enough to take the steps needed to better yourself. It can be a painful thing to look in the mirror and not like what you see, but it is the only way to move forward into the person you would much rather be in the world. The only way out is through.

Ask yourself the hard questions. When emotions begin to rise in you, ask yourself, "Why do I feel this way? Is it appropriate for me to feel this way? Are these feelings conducive to the positive outcome I desire? Will acting on these emotions yield the results I want?" Be willing to be honest with yourself. It is the stepping stone to being honest with others.

If you need to, carve out some time to talk to a therapist, your pastor, or any trusted person in your community whom you believe may be able and willing to lend an ear and encourage you in your growth. Talking things out can help you put words to what you're feeling and process those feelings better. Then, you'll be able to better manage them and any actions or reactions that may stem from them. My own therapist, Dr. H, has been a huge savior for my sanity. If I did not have her to talk to, especially during all of my toxic workplace experiences, I would have lost my mind!

It's important to share your experiences with others. You may find a community of people who will listen to and support you when you are open. Placing yourself in social settings can reward your mental and emotional health. You may learn some important strategies for interacting with others, which will come in handy in the workplace. Relating with others that are dealing with the same toxic people as you or similar situations is very healthy and validating.

Journaling is also a great way to acknowledge and express emotions. When you write your feelings out, it gets the endorphins flowing in your brain and promotes solution-based thinking. Also, journaling will help you organize your thoughts better and articulate them more effectively when the time comes to do so. Writing things out makes them real, and it also gives you a chance to choose how you want to say something or if you want to say it at all. It helps you to think before you speak. Outbursts without the proper thought process can be why you do or say something you may regret later. I would often write out who and what bothers me at work, especially when I could not exercise because of my injury - this book is essentially a culmination of all of those entries combined, and it's been very therapeutic to get all this out on paper!

Emotions can be exhausting. It's better to deal with them than to let them fester. Letting your emotions fester is like letting popcorn cook on the stove for too long. Eventually, it starts to spill over, just like your emotions. They'll begin to spill over into every area of your life and everything you do. Choosing to deal with them is a part of emotional management, and it can positively affect how you interact with others.

Once you have learned how to properly deal with your emotions, you can be more present for and with others. You'll be able to better listen to and understand others. Your sensitivity towards others' feelings will grow as your sensitivity towards your own feelings grows. It will become easier to empathize with others. Working together becomes easier when you can be a team player without reservation.

When I decided to take control of my life by owning my emotions and managing them well, I not only saw how it had positive impacts on my work life but on my home life as well. I stopped bringing the stress and anger home from work, and I could connect with my family and friends more and be more emotionally available. The skills I learned along the way I also taught to my children. Emotional management for children always starts at home. I knew that I didn't want them to face the same struggles that I did because they don't know how to show up as themselves and deal with their own stuff. Expressing and managing emotions in healthy ways is important, and it felt good to be able to pass on these vital skills to them so that could benefit their lives in major ways and set them up for success.

The same can be true for you, too. It won't be long before you are one of the most emotionally intelligent people in the room and by example, you can show others how to be as well. Since you cannot change other people or their behaviors, the change starts with you and how you handle them. It took me almost 20 years, and many toxic jobs to have this actual realization and do something about it. Once you have this realization yourself and master emotional intelligence, you then have to decide to be assertive to keep people from walking all over you. Your understanding nature and empathetic approach do not always warrant the type of behavior that you would like. There are people who take advantage of kindness in the world, and you'll need to learn how to deal with and overcome them as you grow.

Chapter Five

Becoming an Assertive Co-Worker

The biggest difference between being assertive and being aggressive is how your words and actions affect the rights and well-being of others. **–Sharon Anthony Bower**

W ouldn't it have been nice, life-changing even, to learn these life management skills in school instead of 99% of the stuff we don't even use today?

Learning to handle and express emotions is only the tip of the iceberg. You want to assert yourself so that you are not being passive or aggressive and are continuously contributing to the positive work environment you want. Passive behavior allows you to be imposed upon, while aggressive behaviors impose yourself on others. Both behaviors yield a breach of boundaries and are counterproductive.

If you are a working parent, you already understand the difficulties in finding balance and the challenges of being available and completely present in each moment when you are needed, whether at home or in the workplace.

Finding a balance in your behavior can be just as challenging, but it can definitely help you in both your home and work life.

Aggressive Behavior, and Passive-Aggressive Behavior, Is Not OK!

Aggressive behavior is not permitted in the workplace, but that doesn't mean it won't happen. A case of a stalker employee, a raging disagreement that leads to blows being thrown, or an explosive co-worker who trashes the office because they're fed up, believe it or not, they happen in the workplace sometimes and I have witnessed it multiple times.

The health and safety of employees at work should not be compromised because of the insignificant actions of others. Companies cannot predict when conflicts will arise, nor can they prevent aggressive actions and reactions every time. They should, however, have policies and procedures that try to prevent these things from happening and, when prevention is impossible, yield consequences for the involved parties.

The U.S. Department of Labor has a policy that every workplace should align with. Violence in any form is unacceptable. According to the policy, unacceptable behavior also falls under harassment, intimidation, and other behavior that interrupts the workplace environment. Despite this, I've witnessed people punching walls, an office getting completely trashed in a fit of rage, and multiple yelling matches. None of these faced any consequences and life went on, despite dealing with all the tension/drama in the office.

According to the Office of the Assistant Secretary for Administration and Management, every employee has the responsibility to keep the workplace a safe place (2022). Workplace violence and the threat thereof should be taken seriously. Choose to keep your own behaviors at work appropriate and as professional as possible. If you find yourself encountering others who are not being professional, you have a responsibility to report them to your higher-ups. Trying to handle the situation yourself can lead to conflicts that result in further aggressive behaviors. Always know what your job's policies are when it comes to unprofessional and aggressive behaviors, that way you can adhere to that policy as much as possible.

Companies should make their policies known and available to their employees. Making sure that each employee attends conflict resolution training is also helpful in preventing these behaviors in the workplace. If, or when, these inappropriate behaviors take place, companies should be ready and willing to take the necessary steps to prevent them from going any further and ensure that the appropriate consequences are given. Aggressive behaviors in the workplace should be handled immediately and with accuracy. Allowing them to linger, go unnoticed, or unpunished can leave room for things to get worse.

It's not always easy to pinpoint warning signs; sometimes warning signs are spotted and ignored because employees and leadership do not feel like it is any of their business. Getting in the business of others can be a bit intimidating, but personal issues have proven to spill over into professional lives in the past. Twenty-seven percent of domestic violence incidents were the cause of violence in the workplace, about one thousand homicides occur in the workplace each year, and non-fatal violence is experienced at a rate of two million per year in the workplace (The Office of the Assistant Secretary for Administration and Management, 2022).

Aggressive behaviors in the workplace can affect more than just those who are displaying those aggressive behaviors and those that are on the receiving end of the aggressive behaviors. If people begin to feel unsafe in their workplace, companies may experience increased absences. They may also have to deal with lawsuits if they refuse to handle violence properly, which leads to financial issues. A company may also experience bad press, which will deter not only potential future employees but customers as well. No one will want to work with them if they have a bad reputation. If they allow these unacceptable behaviors, people may view them as an unprofessional company. I would consider the reaction to my knee injury from my co-worker to be aggressive, as there was no valid requirement to call me off my doctor's note, brag about coming into work "the very next day" after his supposed 10+ knee surgeries, then rant to me about why my knee was not healing as fast as his did. Perhaps that is why he had to get 10+ knee surgeries - because he did not stay off it and rest like he was supposed to!

On the slightly milder side, passive-aggressive behaviors are usually more subtle and harder to recognize if you're not looking for them or are not keen to discern them. When someone is passive-aggressive, they may say they're okay when they're really upset and then do something spiteful. Or, they might use sarcastic language to get a point across, making it seem as though they are joking but are really serious. Passive-aggressive behaviors can be dangerous in the workplace because they don't contribute to the healthy communication that makes teamwork possible.

These behaviors are rooted in deceit and cause sabotage instead of prosperity. People who engage in passive-aggressive behaviors can self-sabotage because, as easily as they are running from the conversations that need to be had and actions that need to be taken, they could confront the issues with respect and dignity and may get what they need and want in return. Instead of them acting out and hoping that the other person(s) gets the picture. They may also purposely sabotage others because they are upset about something and expect others to know why they are upset. This goes back to effective communication in the workplace, it can tear teams apart, end relationships, and negatively affect the company when there is no effective communication.

Passive-aggressiveness can come from employees as well as those in leadership roles. For example, a team lead could be upset with one of their team members for missing work the day they asked everyone to be present for an important meeting, but they never confront the team member and ask them what happened or why they were not there. Instead, they tell the team member that they will not have the time to go over what was discussed in this meeting and direct them to someone else, knowing that they will not be able to help them either. The team leader does not really care whether their team member gets the important information or not. In their mind, they want to show the team member the importance of coming to work when they ask them to be there.

The team member can be sabotaged in this way because without the important information discussed in the meeting, on the day they missed, they may not know how to do their job properly, as there could have been some major procedure changes. If the team member does not adhere to the new procedures, their job could be on the line.

A memorable passive-aggressive moment was when 10 of us were called into a last-minute mandatory meeting that was right at 1200, our lunchtime. We sent a runner out to grab lunch, and all 10 of us ate lunch throughout the meeting. We purposely did not order any food for the person that called the meeting, hoping the smell of the delicious food would make her hungry. Our plan worked, and she was upset that we were all eating and didn't get any for her. However, we were more upset that the meeting was a waste of time, and during lunch. Admittedly, this was petty and not the healthiest thing in the world, but it got the point across.

At the end of the day, aggressive and passive-aggressive behaviors can tear down any workplace, making it an undesirable place to be. The results of these behaviors affect employees, leadership, and the company altogether. No one is exempt from the outcomes. Employees could be out of work and companies could be out of business if these behaviors are not monitored and dealt with promptly and with precision. Some of these behaviors should simply not be tolerated, while others should warrant prompt action like sit-downs, interventions, and even the moving around of schedules to avoid conflicts.

The Dangers of Being Passive

Have you ever been in a position where you felt something strongly but were too afraid to speak up for yourself for fear of offending someone? Did it occur to you at that moment that what you felt mattered as much as what the other person did? Have you learned effective ways to communicate your desires and needs since then? Have you discovered where the fear of sharing yourself with others came from, to begin with?

Passive people are more concerned with pleasing others than acknowledging what matters to them. Even when they want to express themselves, they fear that if they speak up, something is going to go wrong. There is no trust in themselves to get the job done well enough to see the desired results. Personally, this drives me nuts! If I have something to say, I will say it and not passively beat around the bush to the point I need to get across.

Being passive is harmful because, at the expense of yourself, you are allowing others to walk all over you. My younger self let this happen, but I did not know any better back then. This can cause stress, doubt, manipulation, and disunity to occur in the workplace. When you doubt yourself, others can sense it immediately, and it is easier for them to manipulate you. When you are being manipulated, stress may begin to be a factor in your life because now you may be concerned with your obligation to this other person. After a while, you may not want to work with that person because you don't know how to speak up for yourself and since you can't speak up for yourself, the manipulative behaviors will continue.

It is important to have some confidence in yourself in both your personal and professional life. There is more damage that you will allow if you don't speak up for yourself versus when you do speak up for yourself. Of course, you should keep your communication respectful and professional, but nonetheless, you should communicate. Do not hold back who you are to please someone else if by holding back you're compromising your soul. Remember, you are never too much.

The Benefits of Being an Assertive Person

Most passive people confuse being assertive with being aggressive. The lines are blurred in their minds, making them refrain from asserting themselves in the most necessary situations. The difference between being assertive and being aggressive is in the presence, or lack thereof, of respect, consideration, empathy, honesty, and bravery. Aggressive people are not usually acting from a place of honesty and bravery, as they are not able, to be honest enough with themselves to express themselves in a way that does not require them to hide who they really are or what they are currently experiencing. Both passive and aggressive behaviors stem from a place of fear, Whereas assertiveness stems from a place of confidence.

Being assertive has several benefits. When you assert yourself, you reduce your stress and anger levels by effectively expressing your feelings. It can be stressful to have something on your mind that you really want to do or say but never have the nerve to, which allows it to take up space in your mind that can be better used to focus on other things. Since you know there are other things you can be focused on, you may get frustrated. You may even begin to wonder what is wrong with you and why you can't speak up for yourself, or you may blame yourself for what others say and do. To avoid being stressed because of what others do, it is imperative to develop the necessary skills to assert yourself when needed.

Being assertive is not only a stress reliever, but it is a confidence booster. You'll stop doubting yourself once you find and use the courage within you to be who you are, without apology, regardless of how others view you. You will feel freer like you have more control over your life instead of others having that control.

When you can be assertive, you can save yourself from a world of unnecessary conflict. When you take the time to discuss what is bothering you, instead of allowing your negative feelings to fester, you avoid having an emotional outburst. You will have a more level head and communicate in a way that is better understood and received. Asserting yourself stops you from crossing the line that separates aggression from assertiveness.

How to Confidently Be Assertive

It is not a crime to stand up for yourself, to set boundaries when boundaries need to be set, or to say no when you really don't want to do something (or don't have it in you to give something at the moment). It is important to be empathetic to others' desires, needs, and feelings while ensuring that you are not completely disregarding your own for theirs. There should be a middle ground, a way to reach an agreement that is satisfactory for everyone involved. However, all of these things are easier said than done. Here are some tips on how to be assertive.

Start Small

Being assertive can be scary, especially if it is new to you. Do not try to speak up about everything all at once. If you are not ready to speak up about anything at all, take some time to connect with yourself and get an understanding of why you feel the way you do about certain things first, then determine if those feelings are valid. If you decide that you, and others, would be better off without those feelings being expressed, then don't push yourself to express them for the sake of being assertive, instead, start exploring some of your more constructive feelings. Once you understand these constructive feelings, come up with ways you can express them to others without being aggressive. Remember that being passive is not the answer either; find the balance and strive to uphold it.

Assess Your Communication Style

Do you have the confidence to speak to others without hiding behind a mask or altered image of yourself to be heard? Can you be authentic in your speech without overstepping boundaries or holding back too much? The answers to these questions will help you determine if your communication style is assertive, passive, or aggressive. Assertiveness is the balance between the other two extremes and can be hard to accomplish, but it's not impossible.

If you notice that some of your communication styles are a bit aggressive, think about why you were aggressive in those moments. Was it something that triggered you that you did not yet know how to handle or respond to? Did you wait too long to speak up about something bothering you, allowing a buildup of anger in you?? Had you repeated yourself too many times and your co-workers still had not been respectful of your boundaries? Whatever the case, there is a solution.

Once you discover why your communication style was aggressive at that moment, come up with a plan to better handle the situation moving forward. Understand that everyone makes mistakes, and it does not make you a bad person because you had an off moment.

If you discover that your communication style is more passive, ask yourself what it is that you are afraid of and why. Why are you afraid of speaking up for yourself? Were you scolded for speaking up for yourself as a child instead of shown how to properly express your feelings? Have your boundaries cost you relationships in the past? Do you think that you will get in trouble with your boss if you tell them that you don't agree with something that they believe? There is always a reason for fear, and once you have discovered where your fear stems from, you can find ways to deal with it so that you will no longer be a pushover for the sake of keeping others happy.

Stop Doubting Yourself

It is important to believe in yourself. There may have been some things that happened in your life that made you doubt who you are and what you bring to the table; that made you doubt your abilities. But you are great, despite what you have done or encountered. It can be challenging to grab hold of this truth and never let it go, but it is not impossible. Acquire a good outlook about yourself, and you will be well on your way to being assertive and continuously striving towards mental, emotional, and physical health within your life. You will be well on your way to achieving success in the workplace and in your personal life.

Practice What You Want to Say

Jumping right into a conversation about your feelings and beliefs can be intimidating. Write down what you want to say, or practice your speech on someone else before you have the actual conversation. Be sure to practice with someone you can trust to be honest with you about whether or not your planned speech will work. They should be someone you trust to tell you if it is assertive not borderline aggressive or passive. Prepare yourself for the conversation not to go as planned, and also have the confidence that what you have to say will be heard and understood even if things do not go exactly as planned.

Control the Voices in Your Head

Do not allow yourself to feel guilty for choosing to be assertive. Remember that being assertive is not a bad thing and it does not yield harmful results for either you or the other party. It is a healthy thing to practice, and without it, you may experience unnecessary conflicts, both internal and external. Weigh the outcomes of being assertive versus not being assertive and remind yourself that what you are choosing to do is the right thing; that ultimately, in the end, you will be more satisfied, your relationships will be healthier, and you will experience more balance. Quiet the negative voices by countering them with positive thoughts.

Don't Take Responsibility for Other People's Actions

It can be tempting to apologize for others' actions. Blaming yourself for what they've done or said is easier than holding them accountable. Choosing to hold others accountable for their behaviors can be challenging to carry out, but it is important to do so. Don't carry around the burdens of others unnecessarily, as this can lead to stress and frustration.

Check Your Body Language

Being assertive does not only require effective verbal communication but effective nonverbal communication as well. Take on the stance of confidence. Stand or sit up straight when you are speaking, look the person in the eyes, and give the conversation your full attention to show the other person that you have full faith in what you are saying and that you cannot be swayed. As mentioned before, it is okay to compromise and meet in the middle sometimes but try your best not to compromise your soul and core values. Body language tells a person a lot about you. If you lack confidence in your body language, your words may not have much effect.

Learn How to Say 'No'

This one is probably the hardest one. I worked on this for years, and it is now a perfected art. Saying no can bring about feelings of guilt and make you feel like you are not doing enough or are not being a very good team player. When you realize that saying 'No,' is a benefit to you and to those around you, it may become easier to do. Saying 'No,' helps you not to overstep your own boundaries and overextend yourself. It helps you preserve time and energy for important things. It also keeps you healthy so you can give your best whenever 'Yes,' is the answer. Saying 'No,' may also benefit others because it can teach them to carry their own load, to have variety in the people they ask for help, and the importance of boundaries. Depending on why you are telling them, 'No,' it can also motivate better time management skills. You should not feel bad for saying, 'No.' When you do, remember to speak to yourself in a positive tone with encouraging words. If someone is having a hard time accepting your 'No,' remember that you are not responsible for their feelings, they are.

There are many scenarios in the workplace that could help you practice some of these assertiveness tips. Think about what you would do if: your co-worker always seems to forget to give you relevant information for your project, which means you don't carry out the work correctly. Any time you try to talk to a co-worker about an issue, they turn around and say 'fine,' just to complain about you to someone else. a male co-worker is constantly making sexual comments to another co-worker, but they do not have the courage to put a stop to it; your boss has a habit of entering a room, shouting and swearing at nobody in particular, but the behavior is disruptive to everyone, or that a co-worker latches on to every new employee, asking them twenty questions in an attempt to get to know them. Still, the questions seem too personal and inappropriate for the workplace.

How would you handle these situations? Do they require special skills you need to acquire, or do you think you already have what it takes to deal with and overcome them? Whatever situation you may find yourself in, remember what you've learned so far about dealing with difficult people. Your EQ and assertiveness are key factors in dealing with conflicts in the workplace.

Your Chance to Help Someone Defeat Burnout Through Confidence, Assertiveness, and Emotional Intelligence

"Use pain as a stepping stone, not a campground." — *Alan Cohen*

Right at the start of the book, I mentioned that many people face every single workday with dread.

For them, their organization is a battleground instead of a place to grow, collaborate, and be inspired. Toxic workplaces are much more common than you may imagine. Around 30 million (or one in nine) US workers experience their workplace as toxic, as found by researchers at the MIT Sloan School of Management.

What do you normally do when you're about to finish work and your boss dumps a pile of work on your desk, expecting you to burn the midnight oil to complete it? Or when your gossipy workmate heads to your desk during the busiest hour of the day to vent their problems on you or criticize a colleague?

You know how damaging it can be to put up with others' toxicity. It can leave you physically and mentally drained. By now, however, you also know that you can refuse to get swallowed up by toxic managers or co-work-ers. If this book has helped you gain the skills you need to set bound-aries, communicate with others assertively, and exercise emotional in-telligence, then you may want to spread the word.

This is exactly what many famous entrepreneurs do. They share their knowledge and experience with others because they know that by do-ing so, they can potentially save someone from the distress of burnout.

Grégoire Vigroux, a Forbes Council Member and serial entrepreneur, recently shared the story of how work stress nearly ended his life. After working for hours straight and failing to sleep for various days, he collapsed and was taken to the emergency room. The first question the doctor asked was shocking but telling: "I see more and more entrepre-neurs like you... Can you tell me about your business life?"

You may not have access to big media outlets such as Vigroux does, but you do have an opportunity to help others recognize the signs of burnout and take a proactive role in ending it.

By leaving a review of this book on Amazon, you'll show other employ-ees and managers that stress and burnout are not just "a normal part of life." In fact, these issues can diminish your quality of life, happiness, and health.

Simply by telling other readers how this book helped you and what they can expect to find inside, you'll motivate them to hone the skills they need to be more resilient.

Thank you for your support. You may feel like you need a bit of time before you can set firm boundaries, recognize emotionally unintelligent people in your work group, or refrain from doubting. Set goals for mastering these skills, experimenting with the strategies this book provides from day one.

Protect your friends and colleagues from the devastating effects of stress, too. People spend the vast majority of their day working. They deserve to do so without the toxicity that can stand in the way of their most important personal and professional goals.

Chapter Six

Mastering Conflict Resolution

C onflicts in the workplace are similar to arguments in your personal relationships. If these conflicts don't get resolved, they build up until one person explodes, and the situation is far worse than it would've been had you talked it out at the beginning. Companies incorporating conflict resolution into their training process can see higher rates of healthy conflict resolution among their employees. It can positively impact the work environment for everyone when there is a team effort to resolve conflicts.

Is There Really Such a Thing as Positive Conflict?

According to the Oxford dictionary, conflicts can be described as "Serious disagreements or arguments; a condition in which a person experiences a clash of opposing needs or wishes; an incompatibility between two or more opinions, principles, or interests." Encountering those different from you allows you to grow as long as you approach conflict with an open mind and a willingness to learn something new.

Before now, our focus has been on negative conflict and acquiring strategies to avoid conflict in the workplace. Now, let's take a second to discuss how some conflict can be considered "positive conflict' and should not be avoided but embraced.

When you can face conflict and handle a situation before it spirals out of control, it can have lasting effects for the future. Being able to come to an agreement is beneficial to a positive work environment, even if it feels weird at first. Eventually, the truth being handled with care allows everyone to be free to be themselves without fear of judgment or consequence.

When conflict arises from a place of trying to better things, instead of a place of sabotage and deceit, it has the opportunity to make space for everyone to be heard, understood, acknowledged, and respected. Boundaries can be put in place, and expectations can be set to prevent any future issues, all while eliminating the present issues. Having good communication skills is needed for conflict to be handled properly. For conflicts to have a positive impact, each party must be willing to listen, gain an understanding, respond respectfully, and make the choice to be considerate moving forward.

What Triggers Conflict in the Workplace?

Many things can trigger conflict in the workplace; when you have a diverse environment, there are bound to be differing views, opinions, and beliefs. Some of the most common conflicts arise from misunderstandings in communication. Maybe, something was said by one co-worker or member of leadership that was taken out of context by another co-worker or member of leadership, or maybe, what was said made someone else uncomfortable. If unchecked, these types of conflicts can cause anger and frustration in the workplace, resulting in disunity. Another thing that may trigger conflict in the workplace could be discriminatory actions. For example, if a woman has just as much experience and skills and works just as hard as a man in the same position as her but finds out that she is making less than he is, some strong emotions will arise from this. The female associate affected by this may no longer be able to work in harmony with her male co-worker due to feeling like they don't get the same respect from their higher-ups. They will probably call out their organization for discrimination and inequality.

Conflict can also be a result of closed-mindedness. Some people can be very headstrong, opinionated, and stuck in their ways; If they are challenged to grow or think outside of their box, they may not like this. For example, a person raised in a racist home may have some of those underlying beliefs and may feel that they don't have to show respect to people from different backgrounds. This kind of behavior should be of zero tolerance to any organization and treated with care as quickly as possible to avoid any blowback.

Miscommunication, discrimination, inequality, and harassment are only some things that can happen in a workplace but are some of the main things that organizations have to encounter. These conflicts can result in the loss of employees, loss of trust, loss of finances, and an all-around deterioration of a business. These conflicts cannot be completely avoided, no matter how many classes on conflict resolution or how much preparation a company goes through. They can, however, always be dealt with on their appearance.

Recognizing Conflict Styles

There is no one right way to handle conflict every time. Instead, various styles should be adopted to handle the different kinds of conflicts that may occur. These styles should be implemented according to the severity of the conflict and the people involved. Everyone has their own personality, so the conflict resolution style should also be based on this. Some people only need minimal correction, while others may need to have heavier consequences to get the picture. Others may not need you to say anything at all because they already are aware, and still, others may need it repeated to them more than once.

Do you know what your conflict resolution style is? Does it work for you every time, or do you find that you need to adopt a different style sometimes to reach the results that you are seeking? Take a look at some of the conflict styles below and as you read through them, think of a few times you've either used these styles or when they could have come in handy while facing conflict in the workplace.

Collaborating Style

People who use the collaborative style to deal with conflict are intentional about working together to find solutions that work for everyone involved. They are willing to cooperate and be assertive by clearly stating views, opinions, beliefs, and ideas while also listening to those of others. This style promotes the growth and understanding of all parties. This style is best used for team projects or anything that requires working and peacefully engaging with others.

Competing Style

This style of conflict resolution is centered around the desires of one party. One person is concerned with only their opinions, views, and beliefs, and the end goal is to win. They don't usually care about coming to any mutual agreement and therefore aren't very cooperative. Also, they don't shy away from being assertive, as they want to be heard at any cost.

Avoiding Style

When this conflict resolution style is used, the parties involved don't try to work towards any solution. They just let the conflict be until there is a better time to handle it. This conflict resolution style can cause conflicts to either get worse or fizzle off if one or more parties do not care enough about the outcomes.

Accommodating Style

Resolving conflict by accommodating can be either good or bad, depending on the desired results. If a person does not care about being heard or having input but would rather give others and their relationships with others the opportunities to elevate, this would be a good conflict resolution style. Being accommodating can usually come at the expense of self, so use this style with caution.

Compromising Style

This one is closely similar to the collaborating conflict resolution style.

resolution style. Similarly, each individual's concerns are considered; however, there is an agreement that the conflict is not worth a lot of time and effort, so bigger issues can be the focal point moving forward.

Being wise when choosing your conflict resolution style is a must. Finding what works best for certain conflicts may take trial, error, and evaluation. Understand that even though you can get better at conflict resolution, it isn't something that can be mastered, as you will have to be open to learning and growing every time you meet or engage with someone new. In the workplace, stay as open as possible to solve conflicts as quickly as possible and move forward with the confidence you need to do your job well, allowing others to do the same.

Six Skills to Help Your Conflict Resolution Abilities

Conflict is one of those things you'd love to, but can't necessarily, do without. Without conflict, you may not get the chance to connect with others on a deeper level or work efficiently alongside various people from different backgrounds. The workplace is ever-changing, you have to learn to adapt to the changes, and one way to do so is by welcoming and embracing conflict as a healthy part of life.

In the same way, there are different styles of conflict resolution, there are also different skills that can make the process more beneficial to you in the workplace. Simply put, conflict is just communicating your differences. You may be okay if you have effective communication skills and know when and how to use them. However, if you still need work, here are some tips to remember when working on your conflict resolution skills.

Acknowledge

Acknowledge the other person's concerns. Listen when they are sharing them with you. As you are listening to them, be present. Don't immediately start thinking of all the things you can say in response, but rather, focus on what is being said to you. When you prepare to give a response, think about what you have to say first to make sure that it is a response and not a reaction. Reactions do make conflicts worse instead of better.

I notice that the majority of miscommunications I experience result from people not being present and listening to me, whether at work or home. Most people are in their own heads, thinking about what's for lunch or something bothering them. Communication consists of listening and sharing fairly amongst each party. Be sure to use verbal and nonverbal communication to show them that you are listening and understand. Sit up straight, look at them when they are speaking (not at your phone, computer, or other objects/people around), nod or say okay when there is room to do so, and, before saying what you have to say in return, re-state what they said. Do this to show them that you are paying attention and ensure that your understanding of what they said is accurate.

Remain Calm

If you need to take a moment to breathe before speaking, do so. Do not allow your emotions to make you hostile, as this can worsen the conflict. Furthermore, check your emotions and ensure you are not taking things out of context. Regardless of what has been said or how you feel, w you feel, managing your emotions can yield much better results than letting them run rampant. This goes back to emotional intelligence; When you have high emotional intelligence, you will understand where the other person is coming from, even if you do not necessarily agree with them; you will be able to be empathetic and willing to work towards a fair end.

Remain Present

It can be tempting to bring up past conflicts to make a point, but it is imperative that you stay in the moment. Focus on the conflict at hand. Otherwise, you risk getting off track and moving further away from a solution than towards one. Let the other person redeem themselves by forgiving and moving forward. Think about the importance of the relationship and the benefits of working together versus trying to be on the winning end of the conflict. If you completely disregard the other person's feelings and concerns for your own, it could lead to negative results and maybe even more conflict. Or even worse, the other person may bend to your will and still be unsatisfied in the end, and it could cause disunity and effectiveness moving forward.

Use 'I' statements

Avoid using language that blames the other person when expressing how you feel. To not come off like you're pointing fingers and not taking any responsibility, use 'I' statements instead of 'You' statements. Free yourself from arguing about what you feel someone else is doing or how you view what they're doing by taking responsibility for how you feel and expressing why. Using 'You' statements can make the other person feel attacked and may result in them not fully receiving what you have to say, and lead to disagreements.

Be Impartial

It is easy to have a bias toward your own views and beliefs. However, this is not always the best thing when it comes to conflict resolution. Being stubborn makes it hard for you to receive and consider what the other person is saying. It makes it hard to be cooperative. Your assertiveness may also become borderline aggressive when you do not consider the health and well-being of the other person. This is detrimental to any relationship. So, be fair when searching for a resolution to a conflict. Solutions should not favor one person more than the other unless there is a mutual agreement that one person was clearly in the right.

Be Patient

Working towards a solution to a conflict can sometimes take longer than desired or expected. When this happens, it is important to remain patient to keep communication open, honest, and free of irritation. Remain level-headed at all stages of the conflict resolution process, and you will find that the solution you come to was worth the time and effort put into it.

In Summary: How to Resolve Conflicts the Healthy Way

Resolving conflicts in the workplace in a healthy way, like everything else we've already discussed, requires you to have a connection with yourself. Once you can understand yourself, you can better understand others.

Understanding is needed to come to an agreement and work efficiently alongside others. This means that you will need to communicate effectively by listening, giving the other person a chance to speak, acknowledging their feelings and opinions, and, in return, being willing to assert your own professionally and respectfully.

Conflict resolution also requires a willingness to work with the other party toward a healthy and beneficial solution for everyone involved. It shouldn't be a nonreciprocal resolution. Every party should walk away knowing what is expected of them and what to expect, they should know what they have to give and what will be given to them.

Accepting that no two people are the same and that everyone requires a different level of care is beneficial for conflict resolution. You may miss the mark when you try to solve each conflict the same way. Feel free to ask questions to understand who that person is and how they think before making suggestions or trying to place your beliefs and views on them. As you are expecting the space and grace to be who you are, grant them the same, and if, in the end, all you can do is agree to disagree, at least you can respect each other's boundaries and work together without conflict.

The skills needed to help you resolve conflict healthily and effectively can be acquired. You don't have to worry about not being quite there yet or pressure yourself into getting there overnight. All that matters is that you are willing to take the steps toward healthy conflict resolution and begin taking those steps. Be patient with yourself, processes take time. Be open and honest with others, letting them know where you are so that you can rest assured that they know you are trying your best. You may meet some resistance or come across people who try to downplay what you're doing but remember that you cannot hold yourself accountable for their behavior, only your own. You have made the decision to be great and positively impact your work environment. Do not allow the insignificant actions of others to deter you or drain you. This is easier said than done, of course, but just know that you are not working at it alone.

CHAPTER SEVEN

DEALING WITH THE NARCISSISTIC CO-WORKER

There is one type of person we haven't covered in detail yet. Perhaps the most toxic of them all? This is surely the case for me and the majority of them with whom I have dealt. It's likely these people give you the most trouble, and you will need all of the previously listed skills to deal with them. This person is *the narcissist*. Sadly, the word narcissist is freely thrown around, often by people who don't fully understand the meaning. Narcissism isn't just a case of extreme selfishness or a high opinion of oneself. It is so much more than that.

Narcissism is, in recent times, considered to be a mental health disorder. There are no known and proven causes of it, but there is speculation that it may be caused by childhood experiences, pride, or passed down through generations. Deep down, narcissists are intimidated, scared, insecure, and alone. They are guarded individuals and do not know how to deal with all of the emotions they face on a daily basis, so they lash out at people around them.

What Is a Narcissistic Co-Worker?

Because narcissists are so guarded and do not know how to deal with their emotions, they lash out. They tend to belittle others and praise themselves. They are also unimpressed and unoccupied with the success and feelings of others. They always want to be the center of attention. They require compliments and attention to not only keep them going every day but to make them feel better about themselves because they lack self-esteem. These people find their worth in the world while condemning the world at the same time.

There are two kinds of narcissists: overt and covert. They are practically the same people but have different approaches. The overt narcissist is loud and visible, whereas the covert narcissist is harder to notice as they may be quiet and reserved. However, once you get to know a covert narcissist, you'll find an insensitive, unattached, disoriented, disillusioned, and scared individual behind their confident demeanor. Both forms of narcissists are not ideal people to be in relationships with, work with, or just do life with altogether. While it may seem like it's the best idea to ignore and avoid a narcissist, even these people can be dealt with in a way that can help you overcome them and to overcome themselves.

The Damage a Narcissist Can Cause in the Office

It was so bad that one of my co-workers described working in our office as "living in the Fifth Circle of Hell" from *Dante's Inferno*, which makes complete sense. In the Fifth Circle of Hell, those who give into intense anger are punished by eternal physical battles. Those who are sullen and grumpy in life are forever buried in the mud, choking on their anger. Then, Filippo Argenti, Dante's political enemy, is torn apart by the consequences of rage. And that pretty much summed up how life was in that workplace. We were all angry, felt stuck/buried in the mud, and moving in a cycle of complete crappiness because of one person.

At some point, every one of us told "Malcolm" off for at least one thing, if not multiple things - including rude habits such as leaving his sweaty/smelly workout clothes on a fan that blew directly at us. Or asking him to stop abruptly interrupting our discussions and popping into meetings uninvited. We had an amazing boss who could control Malcolm. The boss could see Malcolm's terrible behavior from a mile away and would immediately squash any of his manipulation attempts. Unfortunately, when the boss retired, things went downhill very quickly as the new boss (then a second and third new boss) could not control him.

As a complete narcissist, Malcolm was clueless about how his presence and actions disrupted and angered our team. In his mind, he could do no wrong, was always right, and thought he was smarter than all of us. Although most of us had decades of experience over him, he accused many of us of lacking sufficient knowledge and being lazy; absolutely no respect. Many of us felt stuck since the leadership could not put Malcolm in his place. Personally, my immune system degraded, and I got sick frequently (pre-COVID), my blood pressure doubled, and he triggered my PTSD/anxiety big time. My colleagues faced similar health issues. He eventually caused a mass exodus, and it was the first time in my career that I filed a complaint to human resources - that job was not worth my health or my sanity.

This serves as a warning for your own workplace - allowing yourself to succumb to anger and negativity can have these devastating consequences. Remember to strive for positivity and productivity in your work environment rather than allowing the anger to consume you, turning it into a Fifth Circle of Hell.

In the workplace, narcissistic behavior could be a scary and dangerous thing to deal with, as you could take hits to your reputation, finances, well-being, and even your job, giving you many reasons to be stressed.

A narcissistic boss or co-worker may woo you at first, showering you with compliments and admiration. Making you feel special, like they have your best interest at heart. Suddenly, this behavior will switch up; They'll start small with jokes about something personal or dear to you. You may overlook the seriousness of these jokes at first. Soon after, they'll graduate to diminishing you all out. You will begin to feel like everything you do and say has to be perfect, in fear of awakening the beast in the narcissist.

This can be a detrimental person to work with. They may begin spreading rumors about you to people who have the authority to help make or break your career, and you may find yourself battling things that are untrue and not your fault. This can also be a subtle and sneaky way for the narcissist to take your position if you are in a position of power. They may do everything they can to sabotage what you have worked for and destroy you. Their jealousy of you makes it hard for them to acknowledge you in public for the great person you are, but deep down, they know it and feel threatened by you. They don't hate you; they just don't like themselves and find it easier to control and sabotage you than to face themselves.

It is tempting to blame yourself for how a narcissist treats you, as they can make you feel like it is all your fault. Part of their goal is to make you doubt yourself to have control over you. It is not your fault how they treat you, and you do not have to give them control over you. To maintain control, it's important to recognize a narcissist when you see one and understand how they operate.

The Narcissistic Co-Worker Checklist

If you are still not sure if your co-worker, or boss, is a narcissist, here are some more examples - narcissists are:

Charming

Narcissistic people tend to come off as very sweet, compassionate, caring, and empathetic. They may share personal things about themselves to get you to trust them and open up to them. They are very persuasive, always knowing all the right things to say and do. This charm is very deceitful and manipulative, as there is an agenda behind it. Now, you can't know if someone is a narcissist immediately, as many sweet, compassionate, caring, kind, and empathetic people are not narcissistic. So, you have to be cautious. You will only be able to recognize a narcissist sometime down the line. Once they feel they have you right where they want you, their true colors will begin to show. Be careful not to disclose too much personal information to co-workers who constantly ask uncomfortable questions, even if they seem innocent. Take your time opening up, don't let anyone pressure you into moving faster than you are comfortable with.

Selfish

With the times changing, more jobs are becoming remote. Most remote jobs stay connected through zoom meetings. It was hard enough getting a word in, in person, but now you have to wait for your co-worker, who interrupts everyone and is always speaking over the supervisor when someone asks him a question. They know it all and ensure everyone, even the supervisor, knows it. They want to be the first considered for any promotions or rewards, so they give no one else the time to shine. When others have their chance, they still must give their input. Being heard is a must for a narcissist. This is an annoying thing to deal with in the workplace.

Unable to Handle Criticism Well

Have you come across that one person who never seems able to take any responsibility for themselves? They may become upset when they are told something they don't agree with or don't want to hear, especially if it is criticism towards them or anything they are doing. They may throw fits, act in other inappropriate ways, and say inappropriate things because they feel offended, even if the criticism is valued and constructive. They may find ways to turn the criticism back on the person who gave it by lying and spewing hurtful comments to make themselves feel better. This behavior is on account of their fragile ego and low self-esteem. They are unable to acknowledge their shortcomings and work towards being better or learning to celebrate them. Perfectionism is their mindset, and anything short of that is unacceptable. Narcissists tend to be hard on themselves in private, so you'll find them being hard on others in public.

Controlling

Do you have a certain way you do things at work that helps you get your work done efficiently and on time? There aren't any rules against doing things the way you do them, and you aren't going against any company policy, but there's that one person who insists that you're doing it wrong and should do it the way they've told you to. They make it seem as if their way is the only way, even after you've shown them how you do it and that it works for you. They may even say, "No, that won't work," even after you have shown them that it does, indeed, work. Not only do they need to be right, but they also have to make sure that their ideas are heard and implemented. Something has to make them feel special and important in the workplace, and pretending to be in charge is one of the ways they can accomplish this for themselves.

Rebellious

This form of behavior for the narcissist makes it easy to pinpoint them. If your co-worker is always making shrewd comments, sharing unethical jokes, and doing things to harass others, they are likely a narcissist. You may find that they disregard others' feelings, privacy, and rights.

Negative

Narcissists are hardly ever positive. They can find the negative in anything, constantly complaining about the company or other co-workers. They will always find something to nag about if they are in a leadership role. Once you do something right, they will go out of their way to find something else you're doing wrong. They do this because they are never satisfied. Their desires are larger than what they feel they can accomplish, but that doesn't stop them from using others to get as close as possible to achieving their goals.

Devaluing of Others

Narcissists want to believe they are the best at everything. They work hard to put out this image that they have it all together and have achieved the ultimate accomplishments. In an attempt to look better than everyone else, they'll downplay others' accomplishments and belittle them, talking bad about them behind their backs so that other people can have a bad outlook on them. Their inability to clap for, or be happy for others, can cause them to be jealous on the inside while pretending that they are unbothered on the outside. They will ignore you, not look at you when you speak, manipulate you, lie to (and about) you, and verbally abuse you to make you feel as worthless as they feel about themselves.

These are just a few traits of narcissists that you may experience at work. Dealing with them can be emotionally painful and annoying, to say the least. They are a nuisance, and, most times, their tendencies are purposeful. However, sometimes they may not realize they are being narcissistic. Childhood experiences may have made them insecure and afraid, and it could have followed them into adulthood. They could have been abused or manipulated in the past and took on some of their abuser's behaviors to survive. It could also be genetic, but they may not be good at being emotionally available with themselves and, therefore, horrible at accepting and acknowledging others' emotions. Whatever the case, confronting a narcissist can be dangerous, as they will more than likely retaliate in the most harmful way possible. However, dealing with them and keeping your sanity is not an impossible task.

How To Deal With Narcissism in the Workplace

Overcoming the narcissist means never playing into their game. Never disclose personal information to them, as this will only give them ammunition to use against you in the future. Don't argue with or confront them about their behavior, as this will only worsen their behavior. They don't like to be called on their behaviors and will do anything to cover up who they are, even if it means silencing you.

If you work with a narcissist and plan to end their manipulative and abusive behavior towards you, one of the first things you can do is begin to document all of your interactions. Document times, dates, and what was said or done. Share these documents with superiors. If your superiors don't do anything to help stop their behavior toward you, you may need to take it to someone in a higher position (M, 2022).

Another thing you can do is refrain from letting the narcissist see you sweat. Do not give them the upper hand by showing them that anything they do is getting to you. They are incapable of being empathetic and may feed off of your pain, as it makes them feel better about themselves. Exposing your emotions to them could be exposing your weaknesses, giving them an understanding of where and how best to attack you.

When you have to work and communicate with a narcissist, be assertive, but make suggestions instead of statements so they will be more prone to accepting them (Shaw, 2021). Since they have to be the center of attention, allow them to communicate their ideas and build on them instead of denying them completely. If you want to challenge their ideas, ask questions instead of making statements. Be kind and remain calm at all times during any communication with them. If they see they are getting under your skin, it may encourage their annoying behavior instead of making them want to change it.

Remember that it is not up to you to change the behavior of a narcissist. They have to recognize their behavior and want to change it on their own. They have to be willing to seek the help they need. A narcissist more than likely knows that they need help, you don't have to tell them; if you do, they will most likely retaliate. So, be honest, but avoid being too straightforward with them. Don't try to make them become better, instead, lead by example. Show them what a disciplined and humble person looks like and kill them with kindness every time.

Try not to take anything they say or do too personally. Some of their behaviors may cross lines and overstep boundaries of yours. Be sure to reestablish boundaries and do not compromise them with a narcissist. If you compromise your boundaries, you may compromise yourself each time you have to deal with them. Be firm but gentle with them. Remember that they are more fragile than they are letting on, and how they treat people shows it. How a person treats you has more to do with them than it has to do with you. Acknowledge that they are human with imperfections and that they have to go through their process to get better. Be patient with them and always remain responsible for yourself and your actions. Let nothing they say or do take you out of character. It is easier said than done, but it can be done.

Chapter Eight

Recovering From Trauma Caused By a Toxic Workplace

E ven when conflicts or problems in the workplace are resolved, the effect of toxicity can stay with you for a long time. It's necessary to learn how to cope with the trauma you have experienced so that you can move on.

As previously mentioned, I struggled with multiple narcissists at various workplaces. At all of those places, I truly liked my job, but those people made it a living hell for my colleagues and me, and I could never focus on the actual job. I didn't know how to deal with them at first, but after repeatedly working with these similar personalities over and over again and researching their personality types, I got a better understanding of how to deal with each of them. With each one, I learned a new thing, and I wish I had known all this information before, but that is why I am sharing this with you now.

I was already emotionally drained and ready to move on after each one. I tried to establish boundaries, be assertive, and stand my ground against them. Still, they continued to behave in the selfish ways they were used to, completely disregarding me and my feelings. They thought that, since they already had me where they wanted me, they were in the clear to do whatever they pleased without any consequence. I even told various supervisors how they had been treating me and how it affected my ability to do my job effectively.

In one instance, someone finally listened, and the big boss moved me to another team to get me out from under that narcissistic boss, whom I will call "Damien." The temporary fix only lasted about a year. When Kevin took his own life (the person whom this book is dedicated to), that was the last straw for me. After my nine years with the organization, followed by them notifying me that I would be moved back under Damien, I could not stomach it. That organization and the job were not worth a loss of life. It took many months to find another job, and when I did, I gave everyone the politically correct answer - that I was leaving the current position for a promotion. Additionally, Damien had the audacity to take credit for myself and a colleague receiving promotions at our new positions because of his "impeccable leadership skills," even though he didn't know we were applying for jobs. I was so happy just to leave that job altogether and start fresh.

One thing I knew for sure was that I could not heal from my trauma while working in the environment that was still feeding it. Can you imagine a world where 41% of the workforce has suffered from occupational PTSD?

It is real and happens when we experience exceptional distress in the workplace.

When I got to my new job, I was sure to guard myself against going through that again. It was hard to overcome the fear of encountering another individual who would attempt to use any potential weaknesses against me, but I had to try. Although I was a little guarded at first, to ensure I wouldn't accidentally share any personal information with anyone who may try to use it against me later. I still found a way to be assertive and connect with my team so that teamwork was possible. It was hard to get over what I had experienced beforehand, especially with the suicide, and it made me cautious of everyone, but it also helped me know what to do and what not to do in my new place of work. Everything that happened at the previous organization lingered so much that I pieced it out in therapy and worked toward healing myself.

What Does Occupational Trauma Look and Feel Like?

Workplace PTSD is described as the "different emotional, cognitive, and physical challenges people experience when they have difficulty coping with negative, abusive, or traumatic aspects of their job" (Beaudry, 2021). Workplace PTSD is no different from PTSD caused by anything else. People who experience it are more reserved, cautious, and afraid. They tend to look at everyone they encounter in the same light because of the developed trust issues. They may be excessively nervous, doubtful of themselves, and worry that their new co-workers or bosses may exploit and take advantage of them. Fear of experiencing the same things over and over again is the culprit, and it can become easy to self-sabotage because of this fear.

People who suffer from workplace PTSD are constantly on high alert and paranoid about anything that happened before happening again. It may become hard for them to get close to anyone in the workplace. When compliments are given, they aren't going to believe or accept them. If someone genuinely tries to build a connection with them, they'll encounter a wall built with the bricks of skepticism. Emotional disconnects haunt a person with workplace PTSD fervently, and anxiety and depression become the norm because of the lack of ability to trust anything outside of the voice they have developed in their own mind as a result of past abusive conditions.

You may see this person shut down at the smallest sign of something being even remotely similar to past conditions, and this is exactly what happened to me at the next organization I moved to. It took about three years for it to get to that point, when Malcolm became out of control, and his actions immediately reminded me of past incidents. I went into shutdown mode at times, and some of my co-workers took notice.

As it happened to me, a shutdown is unintentional and unnoticed because it is a natural response. Workplace PTSD sufferers may not even be aware that they are suffering from PTSD or the effect it has on their role in the workplace. Things can be much better, but they may not recognize it due to increased paranoia. The trauma they have experienced has taken away their ability to think clearly and be level-headed. Their healthy viewpoint has been stolen from them by their abuser(s). So how can you support a co-worker who suffers from PTSD? Or how can you personally strive to heal from occupational PTSD?

Making Self-Care Your Priority

Someone who has experienced traumatic events may become weary of taking care of themselves for fear of seeming selfish. They may blame themselves for the traumatic events and behaviors displayed toward them. If you are this person, understand that self-care is not selfish, it is necessary for your healing and growth. You will never reach the results you desire if all of your time is spent stretching yourself too thin for those around you without taking into consideration your needs. If you have suffered from workplace trauma and feel hopeless, as you'll never be yourself again, please know there is hope for you. There is an answer to your prayers and a fulfillment of your desires. Again, it all starts with you. Here are a few ways to help you take care of yourself and be well on your way back to mental, emotional, physical, and spiritual health.

Get More Rest

Overworking yourself to mask the pain you feel, making yourself overly available to others to make up for past shortcomings, and not taking the time to rest your body and mind can have negative effects on you. Believe me, I have tried this, and it gets you nowhere. You may find yourself deeper in a hole of oppression, depression, and anxiety. Rest is an essential part of healing. It can help your body heal, and it can help you to reset your emotional and mental areas of being. Try to make rest an essential part of your day, every day. Now, I know that some days are busier than others, and getting some downtime is nearly impossible, so it is something you have to be intentional about. If you set aside time for it, for even just fifteen minutes a day, you are setting yourself up for success by committing to a new and healthy habit.

Remember that rest can be anything you enjoy doing, anything that will take your mind off of responsibility or stressful situations and give you the time you need to relax. It doesn't have to be sleep. It can be a walk in the garden, a stroll in the park, bike riding, reading, or watching your favorite TV show. Whatever you enjoy doing is considered rest because it takes you away from the 'work' aspect of life.

Talk to People

Talking to people can be a scary thing to do after you have witnessed or experienced first-hand, something traumatic. You may have a hard time opening up or trusting anyone that no one else knows or gets to see, but it can be very rewarding when you bypass those fears to be authentic. Whether you want to talk to a professional or you want to start small with someone in your community that you trust, talking about what you experienced with a support team of some sort can be a healing experience. It allows you the opportunity to understand your emotions and work through them. It also gives you a chance to build your trust for others by allowing someone to support you and show you that you don't have to have your guard up with everyone; there are some genuine people in the world.

Journal

Journaling is soothing. Like exercise, it can be a real stress reliever. When you journal, you have the chance to write down whatever comes to mind, whatever you are feeling or thinking, and it can remain between you and the pages before you. It is another form of expression that helps you understand your emotions and what you are going through. You can get the thoughts out of your head and onto paper to release the bad energy and negativity. Once you can process, journal some more positive counter-thoughts to those previously written. Since they are written down, you can go back later on and re-read what was written to remind yourself of the negative feelings you once had and how you've overcome them. This will serve as a reminder of how far you've come.

Exercise

Exercising is a stress reliever and my personal favorite. The adrenaline that gets pumping in your body releases endorphins in your brain, which activates relief. It is not only healthy for your brain but for your body and your emotions. When you exercise, you may find that you have the desire to eat healthier, you sleep better, and have more energy. It may also raise your spirits. Since trauma has the tendency to make you depressed, nervous, and anxious, exercise can help you be more present, confident, and joyful.

Exercise is truly one of those things that helps in all areas of your life. For example, a woman disclosed that she had lost her only son. So she made it a point to get up every morning and spend time with him in exercise. She would go for a run and 'talk' to him, in thought, while she was doing it. Not only did she enjoy feeling like she was back in his presence, but she was also relieving the stress of the day ahead of her, all while making sure she led a healthy life. It was beautiful to hear someone have such a healthy and intentional plan for healing and health. You can too. It is not out of your reach. Make the decision, make the commitment, and take the steps.

Find New Hobbies

It can be tempting to stick to your norm, however, after experiencing traumatic events at work or in life, some things you're used to doing can begin to remind you of the things you are trying to heal from. Instead of sticking to a routine, be adventurous. Try something new, such as making new memories with new people. You might find that the new hobbies you take on are more rewarding than the old ones and may even show you a side of yourself you never knew existed. Not only will you get the chance to rediscover yourself, but you'll also recreate yourself.

Not to say that you shouldn't feel anything toward what you experienced. You may never get over it, but adding something new to your life can help you begin to view your experiences as something you overcame versus something that holds you back for the rest of your life. Self-care begins the process of healing as it did for me.

Recognize Your Triggers

An important part of taking care of yourself is knowing what triggers you to act outside your character. Triggers can make you sad, angry, depressed, or even happy. Thinking back, I have been triggered by multiple co-workers and bosses for various reasons. In the case of Malcolm, the way he articulated his words and mannerisms took me back to my abusive ex-husband, and I would have a flurry of emotions - mostly extreme anger. The comments he made, his condescending tone, and the smug look on his face would instantly anger me, and I would snap at him. I was not the only one. I was not the only one. I told my boss multiple times, that he was triggering my PTSD and was the cause of stress for myself and many people on the team, and I requested to be moved. He would tell me that it was impossible because of the lack of personnel to replace me, then laugh it off because he did not know how to respond, leaving me feeling even more trapped with no solution.

It is important to be mindful of your triggers and how you act when triggered. Who do you become when you are triggered? Do you get angry as I do and become someone you don't like or feel ashamed of? Keep in mind that triggers are normal, everyone has them. Knowing your triggers and what triggers you can keep you from letting them control you and enable you to devise plans for overcoming them. Some people choose to be cautious about putting themselves in situations where their triggers are presented to them. This is also a great idea, as it means you know your limits and actively choose not to push them. When it comes to triggers, knowing what works best for you is the route to take.

Meditation to Overcome Trauma

Meditation is becoming increasingly popular as more people become aware of themselves and their need for healing to experience increased peace in their lives. "Meditation creates more space between thoughts and emotions and a sense of self" (Mindworks, 2022). It helps you to realize your thoughts and emotions and to separate them from yourself. In other words, it helps you not to live controlled by what you can't control.

Meditation can also cause you to relive the trauma because it makes you hyper-aware of what is happening inside you. This is the danger of using meditation to heal. However, there are steps that you can take to make sure that meditating heals, instead of harms, you. If need be, reach out to a specialist before trying the method to get some tips and tricks to help you move toward a better you. There are also numerous videos you can watch on YouTube that can guide you in some trauma-informed meditation.

Keep in mind, though, healing is never an easy task; No method you use is going to be cut and dry. There are going to be some bumps and bruises along the way, especially when you have to take a look at yourself. It can actually be disturbing to see yourself in the light, flaws and all, but the purpose of meditation is to help you overcome these pains and fears, and embrace what you see, feel, and think, all while being at peace within yourself.

There are some tips to help you engage in meditation that is aware of your trauma and heals instead of harming you. This kind of meditation is called trauma-informed meditation. Follow these tips to be success-ful in this meditation method:

If you seek out someone to help you with meditation, be sure to find someone who does not separate meditation and trauma, someone who understands that, for someone who has endured traumatic events, they must go hand in hand. If you separate the two, you risk harming yourself, and that is the opposite result of what you are striving for.

Do not push your limits. Know what your limits are and stay within those boundaries. There isn't a timeline or a deadline that you need to meet when healing; take your time and do it effectively. You don't have to heal from everything all at once. If you rush things, you risk hurting yourself even more. Stay away from the false sense of needing to have it all figured out because, even after you are healed from your trauma, you still will not have it all figured out, and that's okay. This is a journey, embrace it.

Choose scenery and places that do not remind you of the traumatic event. Instead, seek out places that make you feel safe and protected. If you need to tweak the environment a little to make it suit you, do so. Do not feel pressured to meditate anywhere that doesn't feel comfortable to you just because that's the norm or because someone else told you to.

Finally, be patient with yourself. Give yourself the grace you need to feel like you deserve to heal and that you deserve to go through your process. Be easy on yourself and refrain from blaming yourself for what happened to you; it was not your fault, and you didn't do anything to deserve it. Understand that you are not the only person who has experienced what you have; there are people out there who have a similar story and have overcome it. Take comfort in knowing that you, too, can overcome your traumas. Also, remember that your healing process may look different from someone else's. Always do what is best for you. Don't rush yourself to get the meditation thing down flawlessly or feel you have to be perfect for it to work. There is no one, correct way to do it, so find the way that works for you and stick to it. Tap into that small voice inside you and change the negative self-talk to positive self-talk. If it helps, look for guided meditations - there are a ton of effective (and free) ones on YouTube. You got this! Be encouraged, and do not give up.

Become More Mindful

Studies have shown that being more mindful significantly lowers levels of PTSD symptoms. PTSD can trigger negative reactions in the brain's activity, causing one who has experienced a traumatic event to have "difficulties regulating and coping with negative thoughts, feelings, and memories" (Bullock, 2019). Fortunately, some steps and treatments can be taken to reset the brain's activity and heal from the trauma.

Mindfulness is a practice similar to meditation, as it makes you more aware of what's going on within you. It also makes you aware of what is happening around you. When you practice being mindful, you take many things into consideration. Of course, as with anything worth doing, it starts with self-reflection. You are encouraged to examine your thoughts and behaviors and work toward having more positive responses where there are little to none. Unlike meditation, where you seek to become aware of your thoughts, feelings, and emotions to embrace them, with mindfulness, you actively counteract negative thoughts with positive ones.

Mindfulness practices help you move toward the changed and better person you desire to be, inside and out. Meditation tells you that you are not your thoughts, whereas mindfulness reminds you to control your thoughts. Don't allow your thoughts to intrude on you. Mindfulness requires being proactive. It requires being more present and more aware. It will take some work as it isn't easy to break emotional cycles and thought patterns habits to create new ones.

As we discussed before, being present can be achieved through meditation, and it can be experienced in other ways. Being active is one way to be mindful. Activity keeps you in the moment and takes your focus off of things from yesterday, tomorrow, or later on. Your full focus usually has to be on the present moment. As mentioned before, being active also reduces stress significantly and has physical health benefits.

You can also switch up your diet. What you put into your body affects your mental and emotional health as well as your physical health. Be intentional about feeding your brain what it needs to function properly. This can help promote brain activity that helps you regulate your emotions and thoughts. It can help your brain reset and propel you toward healing. Couple it with some exercise at least five times a week, and you will begin to see the difference. It will take some discipline to get into the routine of things, but it will be worth all your hard work.

Just as you need to be more active, slowing down and taking the time to rest is equally as important. There is a fine line between overworking yourself and being a hard worker. Yes, do your due diligence, but listen to your body. When it tells you it's tired, rest. Find the balance between the two. This is a great way to stay mindful and present.

How to Rebuild Your Confidence After Trauma

The behavior of others can reflect how you view yourself and your abilities. As much as we hate to admit it, others' actions have an effect on our sense of self-worth. One of the worse things that can happen is someone invalidating your PTSD. Receiving comments like "just get over it" does not help you. Having to deal with these reactions could cause you to question your self-worth and make you more frustrated and angrier. In this section, we will cover how you can begin to regain your confidence after it has taken a hit due to the actions such as these from others.

Check Your Posture and Body Language

Your body has a way of sending signals to your brain about how you feel. If you are slouching, make the intentional decision to sit up straight. I've found that sitting up straight not only makes me feel more professional, but it gives me this surge of energy to complete whatever task is in front of me (especially after deep breaths). I feel confident that I can get it done. The same could be for you too. Give it a try.

Identify What You Like About Yourself

Sometimes when we look in the mirror, the reason is to look at all the things we don't like about ourselves and see how we can fix them. I challenge you to look in the mirror solely to point out everything you like about yourself, whether physically, mentally, or emotionally. Your mirror can be a figurative one or a literal one. Take a look and make a list of all the things you like about yourself, then decide to embrace those things moving forward, and bring those positive things into your workplace. If you start to doubt the areas you feel you're lacking, remember the areas in which you are good enough. Remind yourself that you are human and are allowed to be imperfect. Whatever goals you have to better yourself do not have to be on a timeline. Take your time and enjoy the journey.

Prepare for the Day Ahead

For some people, preparing for the day ahead looks like going to bed at a certain time, picking out their clothes the night before, packing their lunch and putting it in the fridge, and ensuring they have enough cold water to follow. For others, preparing for the day ahead looks like meditating before work, waking up early to exercise or eat a healthy breakfast, journaling, spending quality time with loved ones, or doing some activity to get their endorphins flowing for the work ahead of them. What does preparing for the day look like to you? Whatever helps you prepare, stick to it as much as possible daily. If you need to develop a system, do so. Do what works for you to have a peaceful day ahead.

Celebrate Wins

It is easy to get caught up in your failures. Failures can make you forget what you have accomplished or done right. When you focus more on what you have not done, take a step back and reevaluate things. Begin to write down every time you do something that puts a smile on your face or someone else's, every time you have completed a short-term goal, or every time you've just made it through the day—yes, it can be as simple as that sometimes. This does not mean you must neglect your shortcomings and pay them no mind. This helps you find a balance so that you are not dwelling on them. It also motivates you to make more short-term goals ort-term goals which, in turn, will help you reach your long-term goals. I find it helpful to write down at least three things I am grateful for daily to keep my mindset positive.

Forget the Idea of Being Perfect

Perfectionism is poison. Trying to get everything right all of the time is exhausting and can take you away from the moment. It makes you worry about tomorrow and dwell on yesterday. Try to focus on what you can control rather than what you cannot. You can control your thoughts, feelings, emotions, and actions in the moment. You can choose to be better today than you were yesterday. You cannot, however, change what you did yesterday or control what tomorrow will bring. Stay present, it is much more rewarding and way less stressful. Give yourself permission to make mistakes and allow yourself the space and grace to grow from those mistakes. Forgive yourself and move on. All will turn out well for and within you in the end. Remind yourself of this every day.

Create Positive Affirmations

Some people like to stick post-it notes on their mirror, on their dashboard in their car, on their desk at work, and even receive reminders on their phone every morning. Starting your morning with positive thoughts and words toward yourself can set the stage for the rest of your day so that when you encounter negative events, they can keep you grounded and help you recover quickly. Making this a routine can positively impact your mind and make you feel more confident about who you are and what you bring to the table.

Do Nice Things for Others

Sometimes taking your mind off yourself and putting it on others is also helpful. When you do something nice for someone, it usually makes you feel good and sets the tone for the rest of the day. Knowing that you have the capability to help someone in need, to put a smile on someone's face who was having a bad day, and to share your testimony with someone who is going through something that you've already overcome and needing hope that everything will be okay, are all things that can boost your confidence. So, do something for someone else. You may even be surprised about what other rewards come from it.

Try New Things

Try stepping out of your routine. You may discover that you are good at something you never would've thought you would be good at. you may find a new hobby or amazing things to do with your family and friends that bring you closer together. Experiencing new things can boost your mood and emotions, making you more confident in the moment.

Developing a New Mindset

After experiencing a traumatic event, it becomes easier to think more negatively. In a way, your mind becomes accustomed to tragedy and moves your thoughts towards tragic thoughts instead of healthy thoughts. With these negative/heavy thoughts on your mind, it is easy to bring this to work, and it may be difficult to focus on your tasks at hand. However, this is a normal response, and it takes some work to train your mind to favor the positive again. You can experience post-traumatic growth, which is the transformation you go through after a traumatic event. You can work toward growth by intentionally engaging yourself and your mind.

Start by being grateful. A heart and mind full of gratitude have no space for negative emotions and feelings. Yes, you are human, and you will experience some opposition, but you can control your thoughts and feelings. You don't have to let them control you, and you do not have to live defeated. Living defeated is the opposite of living from a place of gratitude. So, oppose defeat with gratitude.

Also, keep your heart and mind open to the possibilities that lay before you. Every day you wake up, you have the chance to experience something extravagant and exciting. Be open to that. You don't have to stay stuck in the loop of past traumatic experiences; you can experience healing if you are open to it.

Remember to focus on your strengths instead of your weaknesses. Believe in yourself and allow yourself to grow into what you believe about yourself. Believe that you are great and that what someone else has done to you does not define you.

Finally, in your recovery process, be sure not to isolate yourself. Relationships are important for your growth. They give you a means of support. A community that supports, motivates, and walks alongside you in your process makes it easier. You don't have to do it alone, and don't allow a post-trauma mind to make you think you do.

Be Kind to Yourself

Trauma has a way of making you blame yourself. You can become hard on yourself for things out of your control, thinking that you could have done something differently to avoid or stop it. It is important to remember that what happens to you is not your fault. The significant actions of others are not your fault. Don't be hard on yourself. Instead, be merciful and gracious to yourself.

Be your own advocate. Make your inner voice defend you instead of accusing you. It is easier said than done when your mind wants to be negative but focusing on your strengths can help. Be fair toward yourself. Others do not deserve more credit than you. You have achieved much by simply overcoming your trauma. Take pride in that.

Do more things that reward you. If you need to take some time to go to a day spa, hit the golf course, or indulge in things that are cleansing to your soul and mind, do so. Don't punish yourself, and keep yourself away from the benefits of self-care. You are important and worthy.

Do not put what you want out of life on the back burner because of the fear of failure. Honor that you were created for a special purpose and that maybe everything you have encountered before now was a setup for your success. It can be hard to view trauma as a necessary part of the process, and the saying, "No pain, no gain," is so cliche, but experiencing opposition is an inevitable part of life. How you choose to handle it is all up to you. You can let it set you back or choose to use it as motivation to propel you forward. What comes after a traumatic experience is unknown and can be scary, but rise above your fears and own what is rightfully yours.

I encourage you to write a list of ten things you can do today to begin your recovery. Start small and work your way up. Create short-term, achievable goals that will help you reach those goals that may be a little tougher to achieve. Once you have your list, decide the best course of action for yourself. In what ways can you arrange your life to make sure you have the time for the things on your list? Then, once you begin to feel happier and more confident, it's time to pay it forward.

Chapter Nine

Be the Change – Inspiration to Cultivate a Healthy Workplace Culture

I t's not all bad news. Many companies are leading the way in positive workplace culture. There are now 23 female CEOs in Fortune Global 500, six of whom are women of color. Google is one of the best examples of positive workplace culture, with true flexibility, fun in the office, and a huge focus on employee health with pet-friendly environments and even nap pods! Granted, the company may have a massive budget, but the increase in productivity is a worthy return on investment. Generally speaking, making changes to company culture comes from the top, but even if you are not in management, you can still make a difference.

Education and Personal Growth

In previous times, being told that certain training was not in the budget would have sufficed as a reason not to give them to employees. However, now, technology makes it easy to engage in training for free. Millions of videos over the Internet can guide companies into modifying their company culture to fit the needs of their employees and themselves. Employees can also access these training resources on their own. One website an employee can look into is MOOC.org, which provides free online courses. There is no need to sit around waiting on a manager to let you know just how capable you are of being the change you want to see in your work environment.

There may be times when you come across something that you can share with members of leadership, making suggestions that they can then pass on to their leaders. It's important to be the change you want to see and lead by example; There's a higher chance of getting the ear of those in leadership if they can actively see that what you are suggesting works.

Change Your Workspace

Keeping a tidy workspace helps you keep a tidy mind as well. Working in clutter can create a cluttered mind, distress, and distractions, causing you to become unmotivated. A clean workspace says that you are ready to tackle what comes your way. Personally, when my desk is clutter-free, I can focus far better than if it is stacked with paper or other items.

You can also decide to move to a different area, to get some different scenery. For example, if you work in a cubicle all day and the office scene gets a little boring, ask to move next to a window where you can peer out throughout the day. Catching some of the natural lighting outside and seeing something other than cubicles, computers, and desks will help you feel more energized and increase your productivity.

Suggest your office gets rid of the enclosed cubicles to make the space more open, this will allow everyone the opportunity to have a more open view while working. Suggest large windows throughout the office that provide natural lighting. If it is permitted, ask that soft music can be played. This sometimes helps people to work more efficiently. You may not get all the perks that a big Silicon Valley company has, especially if you have clients who prefer things to be a certain way, but there are some workarounds your office can consider to keep the workplace as stress-free and productive as possible.

Take Advantage of Breaks

Get up and get moving or sit down and relax for a while. Whatever your job requires you to do for hours, do the opposite of that during your breaks. If you work in an office, you may be encouraged to go outside and walk around the parking lot during your break–soaking up the sun and getting your steps in. Both things can benefit your health and boost productivity throughout the day. If you work in a warehouse or laborious setting, find a quiet room and rest there for a little while. Taking a break from physical activity is just as important as engaging in it. Always find the balance and utilize it. You don't want to overwork any one part of your body or brain.

Be Firm About Your Work-Life Balance

When it is your break time or after hours, do not work. And, when you are working, stay present with your work. On off days, it is encouraged not to commit to work duties constantly. If the office needs help, every once in a while, it is okay for them to contact someone else. For your own sanity, do not be constantly available, remember that you work to live and not the other way around. Your job does not define your identity, so don't let it.

Outside of work, make time for the things that make you smile, relax, and enjoy yourself. For some, that is hanging out with friends or family, for others, it is having some alone time. Whatever it is you desire to do, do it. You should take the time to celebrate a long week of work whenever you get the chance and be firm about that. Set communication boundaries with your place of work. Let them know when you are available and when you are not. It is okay to choose you sometimes.

Encourage Events

Companies can be assured that they will have a greater chance of teamwork when employees can have fun with each other outside of work tasks. Create fun things for the office to do together during and outside of business hours. Establish connections and build relationships. The more people know each other, the better they can communicate and work together.

Fun does not take away from the professionalism of the workplace. It is encouraged to boost morale and productivity, and to create a positive work environment for everyone.

Be encouraged to help your workplace find solutions. This does not mean you have to present a solution to every problem you see. Being solution-oriented means coming up with suggestions for the most relevant issues and expressing them to your superiors to showcase how they can help improve the work environment and culture. Make sure any ideas you have do not take away from the company's production, and be prepared to demonstrate how. Also, make sure that your solutions do not disregard your fellow employees. Any solutions you present should be beneficial to everyone. It can be hard to come up with ideas for the workplace that will benefit everyone. Still, as long as you and your company are willing to be cooperative and collaborative, eventually, things will work out. A positive work environment is possible for all employees and is conducive to the company's goals as well. Take some time to think about ways you can make a change in your workplace today. Remember that the change starts with you, then take the necessary steps to see that change mirrored in your workplace.

Inviting Others to Jump Over the Hurdle of Burnout

You now know everything you need to know about preventing burnout, and the time has come to show other readers where they can find the same help.

Simply by leaving your honest opinion of this book on Amazon, you'll show other people how to be proactive in their workplace. You will share the knowledge, skills, and essential strategies they need to be more resilient, or move on from toxic organizations.

Thank you for your help. You can stop someone else from falling into the pit of stress and burnout... It's that easy.

>>> Click here to leave your review on Amazon.

CONCLUSION

Toxicity in the workplace isn't just behavior that you should report to management. It's anything that keeps you from enjoying your job and doing it efficiently. You do not have to accept those soul-crushing toxic working conditions, whether it be discrimination or that co-worker that cannot seem to stop annoying you. Changing them is not possible; however, you have to be willing to go through the process of changing yourself while giving yourself grace. It will never be perfect, and you will still have struggles through your path forward.

There are going to be difficult co-workers and bosses everywhere you go, as there are going to be toxic people in your personal life too. Knowing how to deal with them is good, so they cannot crush you in the way they hoped. The takeaway is not to switch jobs to avoid dealing with conflict but to find ways to make conflict with your co-workers healthy and beneficial. Remember, again, that the change will always start with you.

Once you have made up your mind that your working conditions are not ideal, take the necessary steps to be and see the change you wish to see. Begin setting boundaries, communicating more efficiently, being intentional about your work-life balance, and taking care of yourself as much as you take care of your company.

There will not be one solution that fits every conflict you face in the workplace, so be ready to brainstorm solutions and try different things before you find the one that works best for your situation. Be patient with yourself, your co-workers, and your organization. Rome was not built in a day, and no matter how hard you work, you will not achieve complete perfection in the workplace. Decide what is worth your time and what is not, and work on what is.

Now that you've made a choice to take the weight off and uncrush your soul, I hope that this book has given you the insight you needed to make that happen. It is time to put all the tips and skills into action and watch your life unfold into something beautiful while you become the person you have been desiring to be for so long. No more being held back. Now is your time.

ACKNOWLEDGMENTS

First and foremost, I thank God for granting me the strength to get through the hard times and giving me the passion to get this book out, and putting me in the right places at the right times.

I express my deepest gratitude to my husband, Matt, for his unwavering support and encouragement throughout the writing of this book. Your love and belief in me has been a constant source of strength and motivation. Thank you for being my rock.

I am deeply grateful to my dear friends Eva, Dr. Rosa, Roz, Sandra, Debra, Lorraine, Laurie, Linda, Danese, Wendy, and, my therapist Dr. Hamada, for your constant encouragement and for being sounding boards for my thoughts and ideas. Your friendships and support over the years have meant the world to me, and I am so grateful to have all of you in my life.

The deepest thanks to all the friends I've made at various workplaces over the years. Your camaraderie, laughter, and support made going to work enjoyable, even in adverse circumstances. I am grateful for the memories and friendships we've formed. A special thank you to Chelsea and Julia for your positive attitudes, smiles, and unwavering support in the difficult situations we faced together.

I am thankful to my mom (and late dad) for raising me right, and instilling in me the value of hard work and determination. Without that perseverance, this book would not be complete. To my brother Derek and sis-in-law Gail for your support, advice, encouragement, and being able to bounce ideas off you throughout the years. You've shown me that working for yourself is very possible. To my girls, Journey and Maddie - thank you for bringing so much joy and love into my life and being my inspiration.

I want to acknowledge the amazing bosses I've had - JH, NK, and NR. Your guidance, mentorship, and leadership helped me to grow both personally and professionally. You have shown me that not all bosses are bad and for that, I am grateful. Thank you for all the opportunities and support, which also gave me inspiration for this book.

I also extend my gratitude to those who, although not mentioned by name, have contributed in their own unique ways to my life and to this book. Your support is greatly appreciated.

And, thank you to Russell Tanoue for the great author photo!

REFERENCES

- A, J. (2018, October 1). *Don't be passive, it is bad for you*. Medium. https://medium.com/the-post-grad-survival-guide/dont-be-passive-it-is-bad-for-you-301109456f89

- Amaresan, S. (2019). 27 Conflict Resolution Skills to Use with Your Team and Your Customers. Hubspot.com. https://blog.hubspot.com/service/conflict-resolution-skills

- Beaudry, J. (2021, September 8). *What Is Workplace PTSD — and How Can You Support Your Employees Who Suffer From It?* Lattice. https://lattice.com/library/what-is-workplace-ptsd-and-how-can-you-support-your-employees-who-suffer-from-it

- Benoliel, B. (2017, May 30). *What's Your Conflict Management Style?* Walden University. https://www.waldenu.edu/news-and-events/walden-news/2017/0530-whats-your-conflict-management-style

- Block, A. (2021, January 29). *Communicating Your Boundaries: My 3 Simple Step Process*. Anna International Block. https://an

nablock.com.au/communicating-boundaries-3-simple-steps/

- Bullock, B. G. (2019, July 11). *The Science of How Mindfulness Relieves Post Traumatic Stress*. Mindful. https://www.mindful.org/the-science-of-how-mindfulness-relieves-post-traumatic-stress/

- Career Contessa. (n.d.). *10 Signs You're in a Toxic Work Environment—and How to Escape*. Career Contessa. https://www.careercontessa.com/advice/toxic-work-environment

- Center, K. C. (2021, October 29). *How to Spot a Person With Low Emotional Quotient*. Kentucky Counseling Center. https://kentuckycounselingcenter.com/how-to-spot-a-person-with-low-emotional-quotient

- Cherry, K. (2020, May 25). *Utilizing Emotional Intelligence in the Workplace*. Verywell Mind. https://www.verywellmind.com/utilizing-emotional-intelligence-in-the-workplace-4164713

- Clarke, J. (2019). *Covert Narcissist: Signs, Causes, and How to Respond*. Verywell Mind. https://www.verywellmind.com/understanding-the-covert-narcissist-4584587

- Collier, L. (2016, November). *Growth After Trauma*. American Psychological Association. https://www.apa.org/monitor/2016/11/growth-trauma

- Corporate Wellness Magazine. (2019). *Workplace Stress: A Silent*

Killer of Employee Health and Productivity. Corporate Wellness Magazine. https://www.corporatewellnessmagazine.com/article/workplace-stress-silent-killer-employee-health-productivity

- *DOL Workplace Violence Program–Appendices*. (n.d.). U.S. Department of Labor. https://www.dol.gov/agencies/oasam/centers-offices/human-resources-center/policies/workplace-violence-program/appendices

- Dowd-Higgins, C. (n.d.). *Be More Mindful: 7 Tips to Improve Your Awareness*. https://www.ellevatenetwork.com/articles/6170-be-more-mindful-7-tips-to-improve-your-awareness

- *54 Workplace Statistics–What Has Changed in 2021?* (2021, August 20). What To Become. https://whattobecome.com/blog/workplace-statistics/

- Hastwell, C. (2022, March 18). *How Toxic Company Culture Is Driving the Great Resignation*. Great Place to Work. https://www.greatplacetowork.com/resources/blog/how-toxic-company-culture-is-driving-the-great-resignation

- Hood, J. (2018, December 20). *The Importance of Self-Care After Trauma*. Highland Springs. https://highlandspringsclinic.org/blog/the-importance-of-self-care-after-trauma/

- *How to Establish Healthy Boundaries at Work*. (n.d.). Career Contessa. https://www.careercontessa.com/advice/healthy-boundaries-at-work/

- Lamothe, C. (2019, October 28). *11 Ways To Be More Assertive.* Healthline. https://www.healthline.com/health/how-to-be-mo re-assertive

- M, K. (2022, May 23). *Is My co-worker A Narcissist? 10 Signs They Are.* https://www.wengood.com/en/working-life/work-pr oblems/art-narcissistic-coworker-signs

- Mangelschots, K. (2020, December 24). *Difference between positive and negative conflict.* Healthybodyathome. https://healthybodyathome.com/difference-between-posi tive-and-negative-conflict/

- Marelisa. (2015, March 31). *17 Ways to Be Kind to Yourself.* Daring To Live Fully. https://daringtolivefully.com/how-to-be-kind -to-yourself

- Mayo Clinic Staff. (2020, May 29). *Being Assertive: Reduce Stress, Communicate Better.* Mayo Clinic. https://www.mayoclinic.org/healthy-lifestyle/stress-manage ment/in-depth/assertive/art-20044644

- Meier, J.D. (n.d.). *The best emotional intelligence quotes of all time.* Sources of Insight. https://sourcesofinsight.com/emotional-inte lligence-quotes/

- *Methods for Developing Assertiveness and Self-confidence.* (2022, February 7). Live Positive. https://livepositive.space/methods-fo r-developing-assertiveness-and-self-confidence/

- Michaels, G. (2021, June 15). *5 Types Of Boundaries to Start Setting With Your Team*. Trello. https://blog.trello.com/boundaries-to-start-setting-with-your-team

- Mindworks Team. (2020, October 21). *Healing Trauma Through Meditation*. Mindworks. https://mindworks.org/blog/healing-trauma-through-meditation/

- Ni, P. (2015, April 26). *10 Signs Your Co-Worker or Colleague is a Narcissist*. Psychology Today. https://www.psychologytoday.com/us/blog/communication-success/201504/10-signs-your-co-worker-or-colleague-is-narcissist

- Rose, M. (2021, September 4). *13 Tips for Building Confidence after Trauma*. Meleah Rose. https://www.meleahrose.com/blog/13-tips-for-building-confidence-after-trauma

- Setter, A. (2017, August 3). *Narcissism in the Workplace & How it Destroys Careers*. https://www.linkedin.com/pulse/your-narcissist-boss-destroying-you-amour-setter

- Shaw, L. (2021, July 26). *How to Cope With a Narcissist at Work*. https://www.thehrdirector.com/features/the-workplace/how-to-cope-with-a-narcissist-at-work/

- Shaw, L. (2021, August 13). *How to Cope With a Narcissist at Work*. HR Magazine. https://www.hrmagazine.co.uk/content/comment/how-to-cope-with-a-narcissist-at-work

- Sheehan, H. (2021, August 17). *How To Say No at Work Politely and Effectively*. Fellow. https://fellow.app/blog/productivity/how-to-say-no-at-work/

- Stojanovic, M. (2022, April 28). *Toxic Work Environment: How to Recognize the Red Flags and What to Do*. Clockify. https://clockify.me/blog/business/toxic-work-environment

- *Taking Care of Yourself after a Traumatic Event*. (n.d.). University of Notre Dame. https://ucc.nd.edu/self-help/disaster-trauma/taking-care-of-yourself/

- Team Tony. (2015, December 12). *How to Use "I-Statements:" Changing Your Words Will Change Your Relationship*. Tony Robbins. https://www.tonyrobbins.com/love-relationships/words-matter-you-vs-i/

- Tripathi, S. (2021, September 22). *13 Signs That Tell You Your Boss is Toxic*. IndiaTimes. https://www.indiatimes.com/trending/social-relevance/signs-that-your-boss-is-toxic-547960.html

- Vigroux, G. (2022, April 25). *Lessons for entrepreneurs following a case of burnout*. Forbes. https://www.forbes.com/sites/forbesbusinesscouncil/2022/04/25/lessons-for-entrepreneurs-following-a-case-of-burnout/?sh=2ef11f321b67

- Whitson, S. (2019, June 26). *Passive-Aggression in the Workplace*. Psychology Today. https://www.psychologytoday.com/us/blog/passive-aggres sive-diaries/201906/passive-aggression-in-the-workplace

- Wilding, M. (2022, February 10). *3 Types of Energy Vampires and How to Deal With Them*. Melody Wilding. https://melodywilding.com/3-types-of-energy-vampires-an d-how-to-deal-with-them/

- Wooll, M. (2021, June 26). A Growth Mindset Is a Must-Have—These 13 Tips Will Grow Yours. BetterUp. https ://www.betterup.com/blog/growth-mindset

- Yancey, J. (2017, February 22). *10 Ways to Resolve Workplace Conflict: Part 1*. Emtrain. https://emtrain.com/blog/workplace -culture/ways-resolve-conflict-part-1/

About Author

Alison "Ali" Flickinger is an experienced professional with a diverse background in various fields, including information technology, cybersecurity, critical thinking/analysis, writing, public relations, and self-care coaching. As a cyber nerd, Ali has a unique perspective on the digital world and the challenges that come with it. She has also faced the harsh realities of working in toxic environments, which has given her a deeper understanding of the importance of self-care.

Ali's journey has been one of overcoming adversity, as she has survived and triumphed over numerous traumatic events throughout her life. Her experiences have taught her the value of resilience, self-compassion, and taking care of oneself. As a self-care coach, Ali is passionate about helping others prioritize their well-being and achieve a healthy work-life balance.

When she's not writing or working, Ali enjoys spending time with her loved ones, including her husband, daughters, and furry friends. As a military retiree, she is committed to helping her fellow military veterans and those who are struggling, navigate the challenges of modern-day work and life. With her wealth of knowledge and expertise, Ali is a valuable resource for anyone looking to improve their mental and emotional health.

facebook.com/therealaliflick

instagram.com/aliflickinger

twitter.com/aliflickinger

www.ingramcontent.com/pod-product-compliance
Lightning Source LLC
Chambersburg PA
CBHW031419120626
46545CB00006B/2176